THE SCOTTISH OFFICE

D0995039

ANOTHER KIND OF HOME

A REVIEW OF RESIDENTIAL CHILD CARE

WITHDRAWN

21/4/23

THE SOCIAL WORK SERVICES INSPECTORATE FOR SCOTLAND
EDINBURGH: HMSO

SECRETARY OF STATE

You asked me to conduct a review of residential child care in Scotland with a remit:

To examine the current provision of residential child care and the quality of service provided.

To examine in particular questions of training, control and sanctions, children's rights and inspection.

To make recommendations for maintaining a service of high quality.

I now submit my report.

ANGUS SKINNER
CHIEF INSPECTOR OF SOCIAL WORK SERVICES FOR SCOTLAND

CONTENTS

Foreword

1. This report provides a strategic overview of the issues confronting residential child care services, and at the same time addresses some basic issues that affect the experience, and quality of daily life, of young people in residential care. The first two chapters describe the purpose and role of residential child care, and highlight the major changes in its use since 1976. The third chapter discusses the quality of care currently experienced by young people in children's homes and aspects of good practice. Chapter 4 deals with staffing and training; Chapter 5 with management, planning and inspection. There is a short concluding chapter. Throughout emphasis is placed on the importance of the young people's personal experience of this public service, which is perhaps unique in its immediate and long-term effects on individuals' lives.

2. To assist in conducting the review I was fortunate to be able to appoint Mr Roger Kent, formerly Director of Social Work for Lothian Regional Council and Ms Rosemary Langeland, Assistant Divisional Director of Barnardo's. We were able to

    - *examine written evidence from over 100 organisations;*
    - *take oral evidence from organisations and individuals able to shed light on aspects of residential child care;*
    - *visit approximately 20% of Scotland's children's homes, sometimes staying overnight, in order to see the provision directly, and to hear from staff, young people and parents their views on the services provided; and to,*
    - *meet young people and parents, individually and in groups, to discuss their experiences of residential child care.*

3. We also commissioned three studies to build a more comprehensive picture of the state of residential child care in Scotland. These were

    - *a review of the literature and research on residential child care, undertaken by Dr Andrew Kendrick and Dr Sandy Fraser;*
    - *an evaluation of the statements of functions and objectives of children's homes in Scotland, undertaken by Ms Moira Borland; and,*
    - *an analysis of questionnaires completed by officers in charge of children's homes in Scotland, undertaken by Ms Juliet Harvey.*

4. The three studies and their main findings are published separately as research papers. A summary of the review of the literature is provided at Appendix B. Each study has its own value. The questionnaires completed by officers in charge provided remarkable insights as well as important data. The evaluation of statements of functions and objectives is the first ever in the UK. The review of literature and research is the most comprehensive and up-to-date in the UK.

5. It has not been possible to find an entirely satisfactory definition of what constitutes residential child care. As the Literature Review points out, there is no simple delineation of its boundaries, and most authors find great difficulty in determining what is essential to it. This problem of definition is not immediately made easier by considering the position of young people and children in residential care. A child who is not in the care of the local authority, but who is in a residential home or school, would seem to be as much "in" residential care as a child in the same home who is in the statutory care of a local authority.

6. One approach would be to describe residential care as all care for young people and children away from home, and not placed in an ordinary family setting. This would include boarding schools,

all residential special schools and hostels for children attending school away from home. This would be a much wider field than was intended by the remit.

7. The focus of this review has been the 154 homes and schools in Scotland which are either run by, or registered with, a local authority social work department and provide care for the purposes of the Social Work (Scotland) Act 1968. For the most part, these establishments provide care for young people and children who are in the statutory care of a local authority, either through the children's hearing system, or by a voluntary arrangement; their ages range from under one year (though this is now exceptional) to eighteen, and some units also provide support thereafter.

8. In conducting the review, we sought to identify certain principles and practices that should underpin good residential child care, and inform the decisions made about the young people and children involved, whether those decisions are made by children's panels, social work departments, education departments, or voluntary or private organisations. These principles are summarised at the end of Chapter 1. They may apply to the residential care of any young person or child, in any local authority or independent residential home or school.

9. Generally the recommendations made in the report reflect concern at some of what was found but, at the same time, confidence in the capacity of those involved to take the opportunities for change which have been created. Effective change, however, requires commitment sustained over time. None of us should forget that.

The Report in Summary

This summary inevitably omits some significant points made in the text but sets out the main message of the report. The conclusion and recommendations appear at the end of the report.

1. Residential care with and without education forms an important part of the range of child care resources designed to meet the individual care needs of young people and children. Residential care should be part of each local authority's integrated strategy for child care, and should be seen as a positive means of meeting the needs of particular children, not simply as a last resort.

2. There have been major changes in residential child care provision over the last two decades. The number of children resident in homes has fallen from 6,336 in 1976 to 2,161 in 1990. Demographic changes have partly contributed to this, but a major reason has been the development and greater use of other forms of community support and care. Children who are admitted to residential care also tend to stay for shorter periods.

3. The age of the population of children's homes has changed significantly. In 1977 one third of children in residential care were aged between 5-11 and 59% were aged 12-17. In contrast, in 1990 only 11% of children in residential care were aged 5-11 and 86% of children were aged 12-17. The effect of the reduction and changes in the demand for residential places has been a fall in the number of homes. Between 1980 and 1990 the number of residential homes fell from 294 to 154. Residential child care still accounts for some 37% of local authority revenue expenditure on child care, including estimated costs for case work and administration. In real terms the cost per child in residential care rose from £11,000 per year in 1976 to £30,600 per year in 1990.

4. Residential homes fill several roles including specialist care, long-term care and emergency care. Residential schools have their own unique roles within the education system. Whatever their special role, all homes and schools should provide good quality care, support, education and opportunities for development to young people and children. Residential homes and schools are able to offer advantages in providing care and education by bringing together special skills to help young people, children and parents; by offering flexibility and creativity in meeting the social and educational needs of older children; and through developing shared care with families and providing them with a wider range of support.

5. The appropriateness of placement in a residential home or school, in preference to other supports, or another form of care, depends on the individual circumstances of the young person or child involved. A residential home or school may offer the best placement in the following circumstances: when young people need care in an emergency; when a young person needs longer term care and a family placement is inappropriate; when a young person needs care with additional specialist, therapeutic or educational services provided on the same site; when a young person has complex special care and educational needs, and their family requires short-term support in sharing the care tasks; when brothers and sisters require care which keeps them together and when placement with available substitute families would require them to be separated from each other. For most young people in care, however, a family placement will be the preferred option. Children under 12 years of age particularly need the closer comfort and care that a family can generally offer; only exceptionally should children under 12 be in residential care.

6. Placements in residential establishments with additional educational or therapeutic services on the same site should only be made after careful assessment. This does not always happen. The

objectives of such placements should be clear to all involved and the young person, their family and the staff should understand what is required in order for discharge to be appropriate.

7. A clear definition of functions and objectives is vital for the positive and successful management of any children's home or school. On the whole the statements of functions and objectives drawn up for residential establishments are not being used as effective tools in the management of residential child care. All agencies should review their methods of preparing statements as well as the statements themselves.

8. In most homes young people and staff do generally feel safe and comfortable with each other, and engaged with tasks of emotional and developmental growth. Nonetheless there is considerable stress in residential care at times. Staff need better training, and management supervision and support, to handle appropriately the complex emotional and behavioural difficulties, with which they are sometimes confronted. National guidance on sanctions and control should be drawn up after consultation on a draft guide which is appended to the report.

9. The experience which young people and their parents have of residential care provides a major test of the effectiveness and quality of the care provided. Eight principles are outlined to underpin standards in residential child care. These are concerned with young people's individuality and development; the rights of young people and their parents; the provision of good basic personal care; attending to educational needs; attention to health needs and health education; the provision of care so far as possible in partnership with families; good collaboration amongst the professionals; and ensuring that young people and children feel safe and secure in the home or school.

10. Local authorities, and other agencies, assess individual needs, in some cases, with great care and considerable detail, but greater consistency is required. Particular attention should be paid to assessing the outcomes of different forms of care, and to ensuring that individual health, educational and development needs are identified and met. A new series of schedules prepared by a Department of Health Working Party, should be piloted for Scotland in residential care.

11. Some homes have well established procedures for admission and staff training sessions providing good coverage of what is involved. In others the quality of admission is more haphazard; the staff have not enough time to handle admissions with sufficient preparation and sensitivity, and inadequate training to prepare them for the task. In some homes young people's needs to preserve their own privacy, and dignity are well provided for. They have opportunities to imprint their own identity on their rooms and belongings. In other homes there is inadequate attention to these matters.

12. Staff training and support should be improved in order to care properly for young people and children who have been sexually abused, and to care for those who sexually abuse other children. It is unrealistic to seek always to separate these two groups, which may indeed overlap.

13. The individual needs of young people and children from ethnic minorities also require special consideration and staff need appropriate training. The importance of integrated care for children avoiding, where necessary, separate facilities for children with disabilities also heightens the need for training staff in mainstream services to have the skills to meet these children's particular needs and understand their opportunities for development. Such training is ideally suited for multi-professional involvement. Local authorities and Health Boards should consider these training needs for staff in joint training strategies.

14. A significant number of children in homes without education are not having their educational needs adequately met, either because of exclusion from school or for other reasons. Better collaboration between education and social work is essential if lasting improvements are to be made. Similarly collaboration with health services is important in identifying and meeting individual health care needs and providing good health education. Clearer policies to discourage smoking should be introduced where they are absent. Young people, children and their parents should be able to rely upon a high quality of inter-disciplinary team work amongst the adults

providing for their care, education and health needs. This must apply in respect of agency policies as well as frontline practices.

15. Young people in residential care need to be well prepared for adult life and there are several good examples of this being well done for older young people in Scottish homes. Many residential staff are highly skilled in this area of work and several homes have adapted their accommodation imaginatively. The inhibiting factors for staff appear to be lack of time and their frequent lack of training. It is important to support young people after they have left care and into their early 20s.

16. Several agencies have issued good statements of young people's rights. Statements of rights and responsibilities (including statements of rights and responsibilities for parents) should be available to all. Local authorities have set up complaints procedures; the independence of the person responsible for investigation of complaints is important. Young people, children and their parents should be more consistently involved in decisions concerning them, and in the running of the home. All staff working with young people have responsibilities to act as their advocates in some circumstances. Specialist posts may also be helpful. "Who Cares", the national organisation of young people and children in care provides a useful service. A role could also be played by a national organisation for parents of children in care. Local inspection units will henceforth be carrying out annual inspections of all children's homes. In addition to developing standards to inspect against, Inspectors must probe into the daily experience of care, looking for discrepancies and signs of problems. The system is such that young people could be being abused, and that abuse could go undetected.

17. Some agencies and homes are very sensitive to the rights of parents but few have set out clear statements. There is potential for greater work in partnership with parents and scope for the development of the role of residential care staff in working with them.

18. The key to good quality care, with or without education, is the calibre and effectiveness of staff. At present they are undervalued. Greater flexibility is required in determining salaries and conditions of service according to the tasks of the home. The status of care staff requires to be improved to ensure a good quality of service. National training targets should be set. 30% of all residential child care staff and 90% of all senior staff should be qualified social workers; a further 60% should be assessed as competent through the Scottish Vocational Qualification system at level 3. In the longer-term the figure for the number of care staff who should be qualified social workers should rise to 60%.
All residential child care staff should have 2 weeks induction training and new staff should be appointed on a probationary basis. There should be a new centre for consultancy and development in residential child care. The provision of good induction training should be given highest priority of the training requirements.

19. Many of the buildings used as residential homes are inappropriate and not suited to the job. Smaller units in smaller buildings are likely to be more manageable and more effective in meeting the needs of most young people. Better maintenance of the buildings is also required, including swifter repairs. Standards should be set and monitored locally.

20. Children's homes and schools appear to provide a good standard of basic personal care, but require greater delegation of authority and scope to individualise the provision which they make. It is important that there should be an adequate recreation budget, and that transport should not be labelled so as to identify its occupants.

21. Management of residential child care should be improved with clear leadership from headquarters as well as in the homes. The authority of officers in charge should be enhanced and they should be provided with more training.

22. To ensure effective planning of child care services in general, the Secretary of State should, after consultation, direct local authorities to produce plans for social work services for children and families.

23. The report contains 66 recommendations. Those with resource implications are concerned chiefly with the need to improve staff salaries and conditions; to improve the training available to staff and managers; and for greater priority to be given to the capital needs for residential child care. Others are concerned with ensuring and improving the rights, responsibilities and experience of young people in residential care and their parents. The recommendations are listed at the end of the report.

CHAPTER 1

The Purpose and Role of Residential Child Care

Purpose and Role

1.1 Residential care, with and without education, forms an important part of the range of child care resources designed to meet the individual care needs of young people and children. Most young people and children are adequately cared for by their own family and are able to cope with growing up. Some need additional help, because of disabilities or other special needs, their family circumstances, or their own behaviour. For many of these children social work and other services are able to provide sufficient support, in both the short and longer term, to meet their and their families' needs. Others will benefit from additional care outwith their family, either with another family, or in a residential home or school.

1.2 Residential homes fill several roles, including specialist care, longer term care for older children and emergency care. Residential schools have their own unique roles within the education system. Whatever their special role, residential children's homes and schools should always provide good quality care, support, education and opportunities for development to young people and children. That is the purpose of residential child care.

1.3 The appropriateness of placement in a residential home or school, in preference to other supports, or another form of care, depends essentially on the circumstances of the young person or child involved. It may be the preferred placement because of the special skills available in a particular home or school, and because of the special needs of the child or young person; it may be preferred because an alternative family placement would be inappropriate for the individual young person or child at that time; or it may be preferred in order to keep brothers and sisters together. It may be the right place because that is what the young person would prefer. Sometimes a residential home will be the best placement, because a family placement is unavailable.

1.4 The key to good quality care, with or without education, is the calibre and effectiveness of staff. However, residential care workers cannot make effective provision without the support of managers and of other professionals, be they employed by social work departments, education departments, health boards, or voluntary or private agencies.

The Value of Residential Child Care

1.5 There have been long-standing problems in providing good quality residential child care with or without education, as the literature review shows, and as many of the submissions to the review highlighted. The reasons are complex, but an important factor has been a lack of clarity about the value of residential care as part of the strategy of provision for young people and children. Many residential and teaching staff have felt, with justification, that the purpose of their work, and their contribution, are not sufficiently understood or valued.

1.6 Residential homes and schools can offer special advantages in providing care and education by: –

bringing together **special skills** to help young people, children and parents;

offering **flexibility and creativity**, for instance, in meeting the social and educational needs of older children through independent living schemes; and,

developing **shared care** with families, and providing them with a wide range of supports.

1.7 Residential care, with or without education, meets important needs and many homes and schools already provide a good standard of care and education, looking after young people in a sensitive and positive manner. Some young people in care will continue to choose residential care, in preference to a family placement, and their choice should be respected. The place of residential care in the range of child care services should therefore be clearly recognised.

1.8 Some local authorities do recognise the importance and value of residential homes and schools in their policy statements on child care. Other statements have been more ambiguous. Most policy statements rightly emphasise the objectives of supporting young people and families in the community; of providing support for pupils in mainstream or special day schools; and of developing and sustaining substitute family placements for young people and children who cannot be cared for in their own homes. These objectives should not obscure the value of residential homes and schools as positive resources, available to meet real individual needs. Nor should pursuit of these objectives be allowed to result in failure to develop good quality residential child care services.

> *Recommendation 1: Local authorities' policy statements should explicitly identify residential child care, with and without education, as part of a fully integrated child care strategy.*

Appropriate and Inappropriate Use

1.9 Young people and children whose care, educational, or therapeutic needs can be best met in a residential setting do not belong to some different group, separate from others; nor do they fit into neat distinctive categories. Any young person, or child, may find themselves in circumstances in which a residential home, or school, offers the best way to meet their needs for care, support, and educational and social development.

1.10 A residential home or school may offer the best placement in any of the following circumstances.

A. When a young person needs care in an emergency, either because of a crisis in their own family's ability to provide care, or because they are found to be at risk in their own home. Good quality residential care can offer the young person flexibility, as well as support and skilled care. Residential care staff can also, in some circumstances, be able to engage the whole family in working to resolve the issues that gave rise to the need for care.

B. When a young person needs longer-term care and a family placement is inappropriate. This may arise after a young person has had several family placements which have broken down, or when her or his need for longer-term care is not identified until she or he is well into their teenage years. In either case, the young person should be assisted to come to an informed view about the kind of placement that will best meet their needs, and this view should be carefully considered and respected.

C. When a young person needs care with additional specialist, therapeutic or educational services, provided on the same site. The need for these placements can only be identified after thorough assessment, and the outcomes should be very carefully evaluated. The objectives of each placement should be clear to all involved.

D. When a young person has complex special care and educational needs, and her or his family requires short-term support in sharing the care tasks. This may arise when individual or family needs are particularly complex and/or family based respite care is not available.

E. When young people and children require care which keeps them together and placement with available substitute families would require them to be separated from each other. This should be exceptional; the alternative of staff moving into the family's home should generally be preferred.

1.11 For some young people faced with these circumstances a residential placement will be the preferred option. Whether this is so for any individual young person depends on their particular circumstances. Admission to care is a major event in the life of any young person; it should never take place without the fullest consideration of all the factors indicating the need for admission. The personal views of the individual young people and children should be taken into account in decisions about placement. Agency practices and procedures should recognise residential placement as an option to be considered positively, because of its particular benefits in appropriate circumstances. Guidelines and procedures need not, and should not, imply that residential care is some form of last resort. The range of care options should be seen exactly as that; a range or continuum, with different options appropriate for different circumstances. The continuum should not be viewed as a hierarchy - with automatic preference for one form of care over another without regard to individual circumstances. Decisions to place a child in residential care, or some other specialist resource, are important decisions; they may rightly be made at a senior level, to ensure that decisions are carefully made and monitored. Those taking responsibility for this 'gatekeeping' must keep a clear sight on the reality of individual needs, and ensure that the 'gate' is not simply a bureaucratic 'hurdle'.

> *Recommendation 2: Young people and children in care should always have an opportunity to express their views as to the type of placement they would prefer; their views should be respected and considered. Where the preference is an informed one and expressed by an older child it should, where possible, be followed.*

> *Recommendation 3: Local authority guidance and procedures should recognise residential placement as an option to be considered positively, because of its particular benefits, in appropriate circumstances. There should be no implication that it is a last resort; placement options should be considered as a continuum, not as a hierarchy.*

1.12   Making clear policy statements about the purpose and role of residential child care, with or without education, is a vital step. It is also important to be clear about the boundaries of residential care. Residential care is not always being used appropriately - generally because of the lack of suitable alternatives. Residential homes can effectively fulfil their important roles only if they are not overwhelmed with the responsibility of meeting needs for which they are not the best option. Fostering and community care schemes clearly address the needs of the largest proportion of those young people and children who need care, including many of those who have special difficulties. It is not a question of either residential or family care being better; both are essential, and their development should proceed concurrently.

1.13   Fostering and community carer placements represent closer approximations to children's normal living experience of being cared for in their own family. Providing care on a domestic scale, similar to home, can ease the feelings of loss and change experienced by young people, and children during the inevitably traumatic experience of being received into care. This domestic scale and routine daily living are not easily re-created in residential homes, however small. Shift patterns are disruptive and can lead to inconsistent care. Family care is generally to be preferred for several reasons. It can sometimes, be more flexibly tailored to meet the needs of individual children; for example, in relation to race, lifestyle, culture, needs for stimulation or constant attention. Children who have had positive substitute family experiences have more naturally acquired awareness and skills in family relationships, and in the social, emotional and practical capabilities required for adult life. Some may argue that these and similar considerations indicate that family placement should always be the preferred option for all young people and children. That, however, is to ignore contra-indications, which may arise from the young person's own experience of family life, or of family placements, or the young person's own views. It is also to underestimate the need for skilled social, therapeutic or educational care, which some young people have, and which some residential homes and schools can provide. It is unrealistic to expect to meet all care needs through family provision; attempts to do so are likely to lead to needs being unmet, or displaced.

1.14   The benefits of family placement are particularly important for younger children, who have less experience of life outwith their own family on which to rely. They have less experience of relating to adults whom they don't know, and are less able to draw attention to their individual needs (with the exception of certain superficial needs). Younger children generally require closer, comforting relationships with adults on whom they depend; these are more easily formed in family placements where, for instance, the child may always be put to bed by the same person. For these reasons, it is appropriate for family placement to be, almost always, the preferred option for children under 12.

1.15   Data derived from local authority planning statements shows that the proportion of children in their care who are placed with substitute families is continuing to increase, and the proportion placed in residential care continuing to decrease. However, most authorities report major shortfalls in the number of foster parents available, particularly for adolescents. A number of authorities are also experiencing difficulty in recruiting and retaining short term foster parents. The Convention of Scottish Local Authorities, or the Association of Directors of Social Work, may wish to consider the scope for greater national collaboration, to strengthen the recruitment and practical support for foster-parents and community carers. As they know, residential care staff have sometimes been successfully involved in providing support to foster families and community carers and further development of this role in appropriate homes might be considered.

> *Recommendation 4: Family placement should be the preferred option for both short and long-term care for children under 12. Those local authorities which have not already done so, should aim to establish a position in which only exceptionally are children under 12 placed in residential care.*

1.16   Placements of young people or children in residential establishments with additional specialist therapeutic or educational services provided on the same site should only be made after a thorough assessment. Such placements can be successful in modifying behaviour and attitudes, and even though these may not endure after the placement ends they can nonetheless be of value. Some young people's proper development may be very adversely affected during a crucial period of their lives because of their involvement in disturbed or disturbing behaviours. Placement in a residential school can create an opportunity to recover lost ground as well as to provide more completely for their education and development. However, such placements carry long-term emotional and social cost to the individual young person as well. This requires that such placements should only be made after careful assessment and that they should last as short a period of time as possible. Decisions about these placements are generally made at children's panels and it is important that panel members are clear about their expectations and intentions in making their decisions. They need a careful and thorough assessment and a clear understanding of what the particular residential establishment has to offer for that particular young person. There should always be clear objectives, well understood by the child, and the placement should then be focused on these. The young person, the family, the residential staff and the children's panel should be clear what the goals of the placement are and what is required in order for discharge to be appropriate.

> *Recommendation 5: Placement of young people in residential establishments with additional specialist therapeutic or educational services provided on the same site should only be made on the basis of a thorough assessment and clearly outlined placement objectives. The Children's Panel, or other body making the placement decision, the young person, their family and the residential staff should be clear what goals are to be achieved and what is required for it to become appropriate for the placement to end.*

1.17   No single home can provide good quality care for young people in all the different sets of circumstances described in paragraph 1.10. Some of the young people who require residential care have experienced adverse circumstances and unfulfilled relationships, others have special educational and therapeutic needs, including some with complex learning difficulties. These diverse needs, and the behaviour that arises from them, are catered for across a range of residential provision. A common core of fundamental principles applies across this range, but within them care and treatment has to be attuned to the needs of individual young people, children and families. Effectively each home and school must provide for a different mix of needs.

1.18 There is no ideal way to organise provision; local authorities and voluntary and private organisations must decide what is best for their particular pattern of need and service. For several authorities there is a need for a review of the pattern of organisation in order to reduce the number of inappropriately mixed placements; for instance, of young children with older adolescents, or emergency placements and long-stay care. It may also be that some young people are being placed unnecessarily in residential schools because children's panel members and others lack clarity, or confidence, in other local provision which could maintain educational continuity. The authors of the literature review suggest that it might be appropriate to think in terms of clusters of residential child care provision. With flexible definition this could prove a useful organising concept and is commended to authorities.

Functions and Objectives

1.19 It is imperative that each home should be clear about its own functions and objectives. These should define the role it plays in practice, not in theory. Functions and objectives are bound to be reviewed from time to time, to reflect changes in needs, policies and professional practice. Each children's home in Scotland is required by statute[1], to have a statement of its functions and objectives and this statement should be reviewed every 6 months. The regulations introducing the requirement for these statements were the first for 30 years in residential child care, and a similar requirement has now been introduced for England and Wales under the Children Act 1989. When the Scottish regulations were introduced in 1987 it was envisaged that "the preparation of the statement of functions and objectives should be the main tool for managers and staff ensuring that the conduct of the establishment is such as to provide good quality residential care suitable to the needs of each child".

1.20 For the purposes of this review a copy of the statement was requested for each of the 154 homes run by, or registered with, social work departments in Scotland. A full evaluation of the statements obtained (129 statements; 84% of homes) is published separately as a research paper.

1.21 Only two-thirds of the statements submitted for evaluation for the review made any direct reference to the requirements of the 1987 Regulations. The other third appear to have been completed for other purposes, either as part of an internal agency review, or as a handbook, or prospectus for inquirers. Of those statements completed nominally in accordance with Schedule I of the Residential Child Care Regulations, only half followed the format recommended. The other half used a variety of different formats. There was variation in the content and style of many of the statements. Some dealt mainly with general policy matters, while others were more focused on practice, in some cases in a very detailed way.

1.22 The variation reflected how statements had been prepared and who had been deputed to prepare them. The statements fell into two broad categories:

   – those which were essentially documents written by officers-in-charge of residential child care establishments, reporting to their headquarters staff on the organisational arrangements and procedures for implementing policies which had been laid down; and,

   – those which were combinations of principle, policy and intent prepared by managers based at headquarters; these often covered several residential units for which the manager was responsible.

1.23 The length of statements varied; some were brief, others had been clearly prepared after considerable discussion at various levels within the organisation, with relevant matters having been clarified and agreed. Two statements indicated that they had been updated in accordance with the regulations and were based on a review of an earlier statement.

1.24 A minority of the statements provided a clear, positive description of the role of the homes and how it was being carried out. In some homes the statements were regarded as important documents for which staff felt a high degree of ownership, and which were important to them and others in expressing the purpose and approach of the home. However, these were the exceptions. On the whole the statements of functions and objectives are not being used as effective tools in

[1] The Social Work (Residential Establishments - Child Care) (Scotland) Regulations 1987.

the management of residential child care. Their preparation and use are generally given low priority.

1.25 A clear definition of functions and objectives is vital for the positive and successful management of a children's home. It sets the standard of care to be provided, for whom and in what way. This definition is necessary for young people and children, residential and field staff, and for children's panel members and parents. It is necessary in order to properly manage and plan services. However difficult the home's task, and however changing its population, it cannot provide good care without a clarity of purpose. It is a significant failure of management that for so many homes the task has not been effectively addressed, either by preparing quality statements of functions and objectives, or by other means. Local authorities and other agencies should review their methods of preparing statements to ensure that the task is effectively completed in the future.

1.26 The full evaluation of the statements, published separately, comments on both the process of preparation of these statements, and their content. It goes on to suggest better ways of preparing the statements, so that they contribute more usefully to planning and monitoring quality standards of care. If the statements are to serve a significant management purpose, and be more than just a bureaucratic exercise, then they must;

    a. clarify the aims of the home by defining the population it can cater for, and the services it aims to provide;

    b. outline policy and what constitutes good practice; and,

    c. define the method of monitoring whether actual practice is consistent with the aims of the home, and with good practice.

1.27 Young people, their parents, and others, such as children's panel members, should be given the opportunity to contribute to the review and revision of statements. It is an important function of the statements to provide all those concerned with a clear understanding of the home's functions and objectives.

1.28 While statements should contain an element related to education, it is more likely that educational plans are contained, in the case of residential schools, within school development plans.

1.29 Residential schools, along with every other school, are expected to prepare school development plans[2] which comprise three stages: agreeing school aims, carrying out an audit of key areas, and planning appropriate developments. The procedure is to help schools identify their priorities for development and set up projects which ensure that the related objectives are undertaken. In residential schools, care staff should contribute to individualised educational programmes, based on careful assessment of strengths and needs, showing how the curriculum could be adapted or enriched to make appropriate provision for the individual. The school development plan and the statement of functions and objectives should effectively dovetail together.

> ***Recommendation 6: All agencies providing residential child care should review their methods of preparing and reviewing the statements of functions and objectives, as required by the Social Work (Residential Establishments - Child Care) (Scotland) Regulations 1987. Residential schools should ensure that their statements of functions and objectives are integrated with their school development plan. The Social Work Services Inspectorate should review all statements of function and objectives current in (end footnote) 1994, and report to the Secretary of State. The relevant guidance should then be reviewed.***

The Central Importance of Relationships

1.30 Whatever the role of the individual home, the purposes of residential care, with or without education, can only be achieved through positive relationships between staff and young people in

[2] HM Inspectors of Schools The Role of School Development Plans in Managing School Effectiveness (SOED 1991).

a safe, stable and caring environment. This is clearly fundamental to all aspects of residential care, including setting limits to behaviour. A positive care experience can be provided only by staff who genuinely like young people and children and who feel personally involved and responsible. Young people will only respond to staff whom they like and respect, and whose approval they consider important. It is fortunate that Scotland has a considerable number of committed and thoughtful staff, providing a personal professional service of the highest order.

1.31 It is vain to expect that in residential care staff could replicate exactly a parent and child relationship, but they must fulfil aspects of a parenting role for all the young people and children in their care. Basic personal care and nurture are essential for the physical and emotional well-being of all young people and children. Relationships are a key factor in all aspects of development. Children with special educational needs, for instance, depend heavily on relationships in the development of their communication skills, which are often crucial to their capacity to develop. It is important that each young person and child with emotional and behavioural difficulties has a sense of being liked and valued - even when her or his behaviour is not. Without these there is no possibility of meeting social and developmental needs, or of helping to deal with the damaging experiences that many have had. As one respondent commented, "children who have experienced damage in their primary relationships have developed an internal sense of their inability to sustain positive relationships with primary carers". In short, they often feel not good enough to be cared about. Residential staff have no mean task in working to repair this damage but at the same time avoiding re-creating the damaging situation.

1.32 The kind of relationships young people and children need in order to develop their full potential are not easily formed and maintained. They need opportunities to develop positive relationships with their peers and adults, and these require a high level of skill and understanding. The emphasis on the importance of relationships in residential child care seems obvious, but must not be taken for granted. Statements of functions and objectives should be conceived, planned, expressed and developed in ways that reflect the central importance of the relationships between staff and young people and children, and which emphasise the young person's or child's experience of care. Young people, their parents and staff should be able to have clear expectations of residential care.

What Young People Should Be Able To Expect

1.33 Regardless of how long or short a time a young person or child is cared for in a residential home or unit, her or his basic emotional, physical and developmental needs, and rights as an individual, must be recognised, and effectively addressed. Though it may not be their true "home" in every sense of that word, it is much more than somewhere they "attend", like a day school or an Intermediate Treatment group. It is where they live, and certain expectations follow. Young people and children should expect:

- Their rights to be respected.

- Their parents' rights to be respected and, wherever possible, their parents' involvement as partners in the care provided.

- To be treated with respect and dignity; to be treated as individuals with their own unique relationships, experiences, strengths, needs and futures.

- To participate in the decisions that affect them, and those that effect the running of the home or school.

- To feel safe and secure in the home or school.

- To have privacy, and dignity; with special regard paid to this when they need personal care.

- Each to have a "special person" to relate to during the time they live in the home or school; and to be able to talk to that person in confidence.

- To be protected from harm, including self-harm.

- To have appropriate limits set on their behaviour.

- To be well looked after physically; to be comfortable and well fed.

- Their health to be given individual attention.

- To be actively encouraged in their formal education and, as they get older, in further education, vocational training or employment.

- To have new, varied and positive experiences.

- To learn how to look after themselves in a practical way, and to be assisted to develop the common skills required of adults.

- To have the opportunity to work on emotional issues when they need to.

- To be admitted to the home or school in a planned and sensitive way.

- To move on to well-planned situations.

- To be fully and carefully prepared for any move out of the home or school, whether back to their own home, to some other form of care, or to independent living.

A Set of Fundamental Principles

1.34 These expectations can be expressed in the eight principles for underpinning residential child care listed below. These have been drawn up with particular regard to young people's experience of care. They provide a framework within which relevant standards for evaluating the quality of residential child care may be better developed.

I. INDIVIDUALITY AND DEVELOPMENT

Young people and children in residential care have the right to be treated as individuals who have their own unique relationships, experiences, strengths, needs and futures, irrespective of the needs of other residents. They should be prepared for adulthood and supported until they are fully independent.

II. RIGHTS AND RESPONSIBILITIES

Young people, children and their parents should be given a clear statement of their rights and responsibilities. They should have a confidential means of making complaints. They should be involved in decisions affecting them and in the running of the home. Their rights should be consistently respected.

III. GOOD BASIC CARE

Young people and children in residential care with or without education, should be given a high standard of personal care. They should be offered new, varied and positive experiences of life and should be included in the wider community

IV. EDUCATION

Young people and children should be actively encouraged in all aspects of their education, vocational training or employment and offered career guidance. Their individual educational needs should be identified and met.

V. HEALTH

Young people's and children's health needs should be carefully identified and met; they should be encouraged to avoid health risks and to develop a healthy life-style.

VI. PARTNERSHIPS WITH PARENTS

Young people and children in residential homes and schools should be cared for in ways which maximise opportunities for parents continued involvement, and for care to be provided in the context of a partnership with parents, wherever this is in the interests of the child.

VII. CHILD CENTRED COLLABORATION

Young people and children should be able to rely on a high quality of inter-disciplinary teamwork amongst the adults providing for their care, education and health needs.

VIII. A FEELING OF SAFETY

Young people and children should feel safe and secure in any residential home or school.

> *Recommendation 7: The Social Work Services Inspectorate, in consultation with local authorities and other agencies, should further develop standards and guidance for evaluating residential child care within the framework of the eight principles outlined in this report and, as appropriate, other identified areas. The development of these standards should draw on analysis of the experiences of young people, children and their parents. The standards should be applied by managers and local inspection units to ensure a consistently good quality of residential child care provision.*

1.35 These eight principles provide the framework for Chapter 3, in which the quality of residential child care currently provided is considered, together with aspects of good practice. Over the last two decades there have been major changes in residential child care and these are described in Chapter 2.

CHAPTER 2

The Decades of Change

2.1 Over the 1970s and 1980s residential provision for children in care in Scotland changed dramatically. Before considering aspects of residential child care in more detail, it is important to note the broad changes which have shaped the present pattern of services.

The Fall In The Number Of Residents

2.2 The number of young people and children resident in homes and schools run by, or registered with, social work departments fell from 6,336 in 1976 to 2,161 in 1990 - a third of the 1976 level. During this period there was a general reduction in the size of the population aged 0-17, but the reduction in the number of children in residential care was greater than could have been predicted from population changes alone. It reflects the impact of policy and practice changes including the increased level of alternative support for young people and children through, for instance, family centres, intermediate treatment projects and fostering and community caring schemes. Figure 1 shows the proportion of the total Scottish population aged 0-17 in residential care for each of the years 1980 to 1990; during these years the proportion fell from 4.2 per thousand to 2.0 per thousand.

Figure 1: Children in Residential Care as a Proportion of Population of All Children 1980-1990.

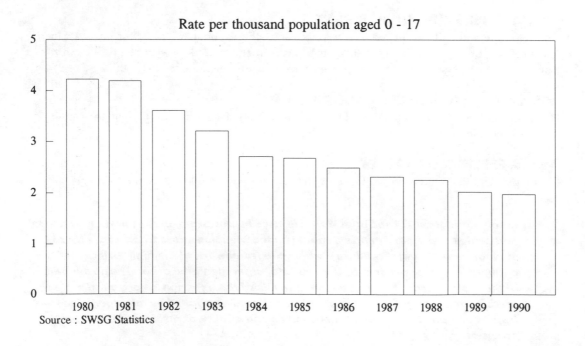

Rate per thousand population aged 0 - 17

Source : SWSG Statistics

2.3 Children in care or under supervision may be placed in residential care, with foster-parents or community carers, or supervised at home. Between 1980 and 1990 the total number of children in care or under supervision fell from 16,845 to 13,052 (that is by 23%). However, the population aged 0-17 also fell during this period, and the proportion of that population which was in care or under supervision, in the end, changed only slightly. The proportion in care, or under supervision, declined from 11.8 per thousand aged 0-17 in 1980 to around 10.4 per thousand in the late 80s, and was 11.3 per thousand in 1990. Early indications for 1991 show little overall change in the number of children in care or under supervision.

2.4   There are significant regional variations within these figures. For Strathclyde the 1980 figure was 13.1 per thousand, during the 1980s it varied between 13.1 and 14.5 per thousand, and the 1990 figure was 15.0 per thousand. The Lothian figure fell from 12.7 per thousand in 1980 to 7.7 per thousand in 1985, before rising to 8.9 per thousand in 1990. The figure for Fife, which was 9.1 in 1980, fell steadily over the decade reaching 3.4 per thousand, in 1989, and was 4.4 in 1990.

2.5   Of the total number of children in care or under supervision there was, during the 1980s, a significant reduction in the proportion who were in residential care. This is demonstrated in Figure 2, which shows the proportions of children, in care or under supervision, who were at home, in residential care or in foster care. Prior to 1984 the figures for children in foster care were not separated from those living with relatives or friends, and therefore the proportion in foster care prior to 1984 is not shown separately. The proportion at home, and the proportion in residential care, are both comparable across the decade; Figure 2 shows that whilst the proportion at home went up, the proportion in residential care went down. These changes were continuations of trends which started in the 1970s. Whereas in 1976 36% of children in local authority care were placed in residential establishments, this had fallen to 18% in 1990. Early indications for 1991 show a further slight fall in the proportion of children in care or under supervision who were in residential care.

Figure 2: Children in Care or Under Supervision (1980-90)

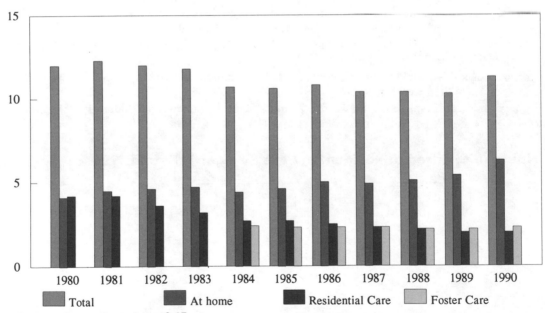

Rate per thousand population 0-17
Source: SWSG Statistics

2.6   This reduction in the proportion of children in care or under supervision who are in residential care, has not been uniform across Scotland. There are regional variations, both in the changes over the last decade, and in the proportion of children in residential care. Figure 3 shows the regional variation in 1990 in the proportion of children in care or under supervision who were in residential care.

Figure 3: Children in Residential Care as Percentage of Total Number of Children in Care by Region: 1990

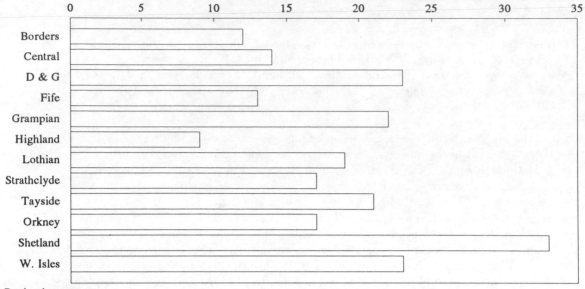

Region by percentage
Source : SWSG Statistics

Changes In the Ages of Residents

2.7 Within the overall reduction in the numbers in residential care there were significant differences in the amount of reduction for different age groups. In 1977 41% of all children in care aged less than 12 were in residential establishments; this proportion had declined to 6% in 1990. In 1977 34% of all children in care aged 12-17 year old were in residential care; this proportion had declined to 27% in 1990. This has meant that the population of children's homes has changed significantly. In 1977 one-third of children in residential care were aged between 5 and 11, and 59% were aged 12-17. In contrast, in 1990 only 11% of children in residential care were aged 5-11, and 86% of children were aged 12-17.

Figure 3 shows the comparisons between 1977 and 1990 of the numbers of children in residential care, for each of three age groups: 0-4, 5-11 and 12-17.

Figure 4: Children in Residential Care By Age: 1977 and 1990.

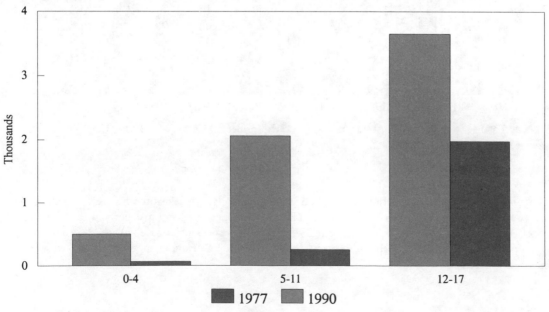

Ages by Numbers (in thousands)
Source: SWSG Statistics

2.8   When the ages of children in residential care are examined, significant regional variations are found. For example, 13% of children in residential care in Strathclyde in 1990 were aged 10 or younger, 2% of children in residential care in Lothian in 1990 were aged 10 or younger and Borders and Fife had no children aged 10 or younger in residential care. Figure 5 shows, for each region, the proportion of children in residential care aged 0-10, 11-15 and 16 plus.

Figure 5: Regional Age Profiles of Children in Residential Establishments 1990.

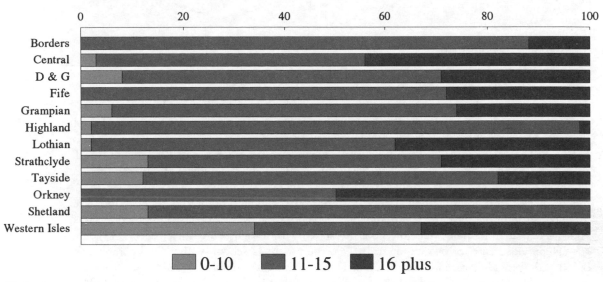

Region by percentages
Source : SWSG Statistics

Changes in Statutory Basis And Duration of Placement

2.9   There have also been changes in the statutory care status of children in residential homes, though less change in respect of children in care in residential schools. Generally children may come into care either through the children's hearing system, when they are made the subject of a statutory residential or non-residential supervision requirement, or through a voluntary arrangement between the parents and the local authority. In 1977 45% of all children in care were in care on a voluntary basis, whereas in 1990 the comparable figure was only 13%. In 1977 39% of all children in residential care were subject to a residential supervision requirement made by a Children's Hearing; in 1990 54% of children in residential care were subject to such a requirement. In 1977 around 23% of children in local authority residential homes were there on the basis of a residential supervision order; in 1990 this proportion had risen to 51%.

2.10   The duration of children's and young people's placement in residential establishments has changed significantly over these two decades. Figures for the 1970s and early 1980s are not available, but probably the greatest changes occurred during those years. Figures are available for the years 1986 to 1990 and these are contained in Table 1. These show a trend for a greater proportion of children who are admitted to residential care, to remain in care for shorter periods of time. The proportion remaining in residential care for three years or more fell from 31% in 1986 to 24% in 1990.

Table 1: Lengths of Stay in Residential Care: Percentage Distribution 1986 to 1990					
	1986	1987	1988	1989	1990
	%	%	%	%	%
0-6 mths	24	21	21	23	26
6 mths-1 yr	15	17	14	16	16
1-3 yrs	30	33	36	34	34
3+ yrs	31	30	29	27	24
Total No (=100%)	3060	2784	2664	2364	2296

Source: SWSG Statistics

Changes in the Number, Occupancy and Size of Homes

2.11   The effect of the reduction and changes in the demand for residential places has been a fall in the number of homes and places. Between 1980 and 1990 the number of residential homes fell from 294 to 154 (52% of the 1980 level). The total bed complement reduced over this period from 6558 beds to 2701 beds (41% of the 1980 level). Figure 6 shows, for the years 1980 to 1990, both the number of beds in residential establishments in Scotland and the number of children resident. The figure illustrates the reduction in both of these figures. Since 1987 the gap between the number of residents and the number of beds has narrowed and both of their rates of decline have lessened. In 1986 the separate organisation and categorisation of "List D" residential schools was ended. At that time there were 16 schools registered with a total bed capacity of 857, which on average provided care for 645 children. In 1990 there were 12 schools with a total complement of 591 beds, providing care for 500 children. The decrease in the number of beds in the voluntary and private sector (54%) has been more marked than that in the local authority sector (42%). As well as reducing in number voluntary sector homes have generally become more specialised in the children for whom they provide care.

Figure 6: Residential Establishments for Children 1980 to 1990: Bed Complement and Residents

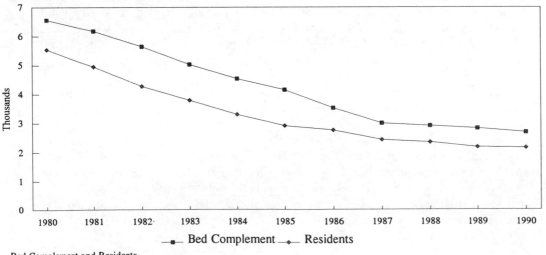

Bed Complement and Residents
Source : SWSG Statistics

2.12   Occupancy rates have varied over the past two decades, as the demand for places, and the number of places provided have both changed. Overall occupancy levels fell from 90% in 1976 to 75% in 1983 representing at that time 1,246 unfilled places. Statistical returns since 1983 show occupancy levels rose to 80% in 1990. The survey conducted for this review found an average occupancy of 87% in 1991.

2.13   There are significant regional variations within this national picture. Figure 7 shows, for each region, the percentage of available beds which were occupied in 1990. The figures from which the graph is drawn include all homes and schools provided by, or registered with, local social work departments.

Figure 7: Occupancy Rates For Residential Care: 1990.

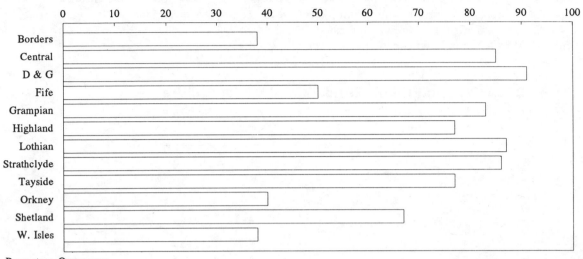

Percentage Occupancy
Source : SWSG Statistics

2.14   Statistics for 1990 showed that the bulk of residential homes (57%) have 9 to 23 beds; 17% of homes have 24 or more beds; and 26% of homes were relatively small, being established for 8 or fewer beds. This is shown in Table 2.

Table 2: Size of Residential Homes: 1990

	Up to 8	9-23	24+	Total
Number of Homes	40	88	26	154

Source: SWSG Statistics

2.15   The larger homes, of course, cater for more children and the proportion of children living in small homes remains much smaller than the number of small homes might initially suggest. This is shown in Table 3.

Table 3: Children Living in Homes of Different Sizes 1990

Size of Home				
	8 or less	9-23	24	Total
Number of Children	210	1143	897	2250
% of all in Resid.Care	9%	51%	40%	100

Source: SWSG Statistics

Changes In Finance

2.16 Although the number of children in residential care has fallen, the costs of providing, or purchasing, residential care for children remain very significant. In 1977 local authority expenditure on residential care for children was, at 1991 prices, £70 million; in 1991 it was £63 million. In real terms, local authority total expenditure on residential child care has fallen by about 10% since 1976; the number of children by 60%. After rising significantly in the late seventies, the total cost of residential child care gradually fell back during the eighties. These costs, and the figures which follow, include both the costs of direct provision and the costs of supporting places in the private and voluntary sectors. Figure 8 shows the changes in local authority total expenditure on residential care for children between 1977 and 1990, and shows both actual expenditure, and expenditure converted to 1991 prices.

Figure 8: LA Expenditure on Residential Care for Children 1977-1990

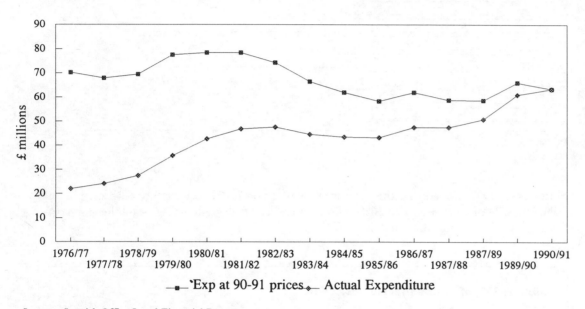

Source : Scottish Office Local Financial Returns

2.17 Residential child care also remains a very significant proportion of all local authority social work expenditure on child care. Residential care accounts for 55% of the identified expenditure on child care by local authorities in Scotland. A significant element of expenditure by local authorities on child care is contained under the budget heads for casework and administration, which are not allowed for in the identified figure. In 1991 the Scottish Office published a study of the distribution of casework and administrative time spent in relation to different client groups[3]. An estimate of how much of this expenditure on casework and administration should be allocated to child care can be made from this study. Making allowance for this element provides a more accurate picture. On this calculation, residential care accounts for 37% of local authority expenditure on child care.

2.18 Figure 9 shows, for each authority, expenditure on residential care as a percentage of total expenditure on child care, identified by the local authority financial returns, and including an additional estimate for the amount of unallocated casework and central administration incurred in relation to child care. The figure shows that regional variations are significant, and that for all authorities residential child care remains a major element of child care expenditure.

[3] "Where The Time Goes", The Scottish Office, 1992.

Figure 9: Expenditure on Residential Care as Percentage of LA Expenditure on Children (Including unallocated expenditure) 1990/91.

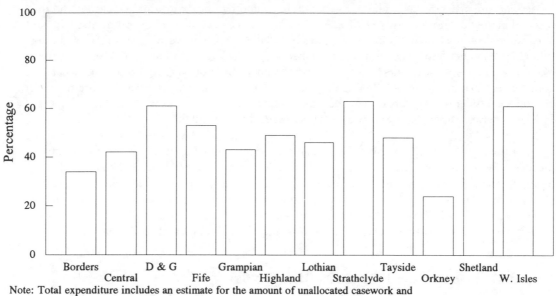

Note: Total expenditure includes an estimate for the amount of unallocated casework and central administration expenditure incurred on child care

2.19   The expenditure per child in residential care has risen significantly. In 1976 the expenditure per child in residential care was, at 1991 prices, £11,000 per year. In 1990 it was £30,600 per child per year. Figure 10 shows the expenditure per child in residential care for each year from 1977 to 1990. These figures have been calculated by dividing the total expenditure on residential child care (given through the local financial returns) by the numbers of children in residential care (provided in the SWSG Statistics).

Figure 10: Expenditure Per Child in Residential Care

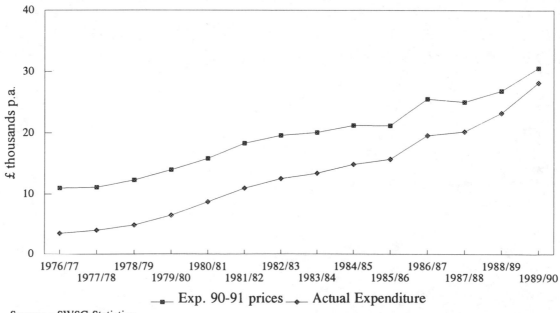

— Exp. 90-91 prices — Actual Expenditure

Sources : SWSG Statistics
         Scottish Office Local Financial Returns

Summary

2.20 Residential child care has undergone major changes. Over the last two decades there has been a significant fall in the numbers of children in residential care. The proportion of children in residential care may now be levelling out, but there remain significant regional variations and the national picture cannot be easily predicted. There has been a fall and levelling out in the number of residential establishments. Occupancy rates have fallen and then risen again. The number of children aged under 5 in residential care has fallen very considerably and remained very low; the use of residential care for children aged between 5 and 12 has not fallen quite so much, but nonetheless the numbers have fallen significantly, and remained at a lower level. Despite the drop in numbers residential child care remains a major element in any authority's child care budget. The costs per child per year have risen 3-fold between 1976 and 1990.

2.21 Many of the changes may be attributable to changes in policy and practice, however the past two decades have seen significant demographic changes which have not only caused some of the changes, but have also presented a rather turbulent environment for managing the changes in practice. Population projections for the next decade, up to the end of the century, present a more stable pattern. This is shown in Figure 12. This shows, for Scotland as a whole, the changes in the numbers in each of three age bands; 0-4 years old, 5-9 years old and 15-19 years old.

Figure 11: Population 1970-2000 (Under 20s)

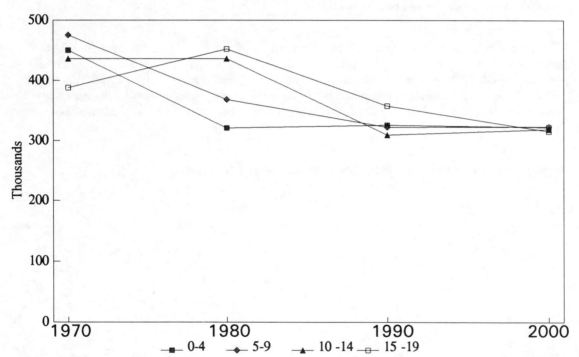

Base : 1989 Population
Source : General Register Office (Scotland)

CHAPTER 3

The Quality of Care

3.1 To fulfil the remit an appraisal of the strengths and weaknesses of the general quality of care being experienced by young people and children in homes in Scotland was required. The commentary in this chapter is drawn from visits to homes, from discussions with young people, children and their parents, from the written and oral submissions made to the review, as well as from the survey returns, the literature review and the evaluation of statements. This chapter follows the headings of the eight principles outlined in Chapter 1; aspects of good practice are discussed, as well as comments on current provision.

I. INDIVIDUALITY AND DEVELOPMENT

Young people and children in residential care have the right to be treated as individuals who have their own unique relationships, experiences, strengths, needs and futures, irrespective of the needs of other residents. They should be prepared for adulthood and supported until they are fully independent.

3.1.1 Treating each young person or child as an individual is central to all good child care. For young people and children residential care is not a system, or a service; it is a unique and profound personal experience which will have lasting effects and impressions, for good or ill, throughout the rest of their lives.

Admissions

3.1.2 Local social work authorities and other agencies place considerable emphasis in their policies and procedures on the importance of preventing admission to care and particularly to residential care. They are right to do so and in this their policies follow the framework of the Social Work (Scotland) Act 1968. Earlier admissions seem unlikely to lead to better outcomes. However, for those admitted to care preparation is as important as prevention is for those who are not.

3.1.3 Where admission is required the way into residential care should be well prepared, through careful planning of the admission and arrangements for pre-admission visits. In practice, however, such preparation is the exception rather than the rule. The majority of young people are only briefly prepared. Many young people and children are admitted in an emergency, and in these circumstances preparation is difficult. The main problem appears to be the lack of time which is made available to prepare young people. Residential staff would be able to play a greater role in this, as they already do in some homes, if staffing levels and shift systems permitted.

3.1.4 The young person's preparation for, and introduction to, a home is likely to play an important part in how she or he establishes relationships thereafter. As residential staff recognise well, coming into care can be the loneliest moment in the young person's life, and it needs to be handled in a calm, positive and reassuring way. The circumstances of the admission, the attitude of the young person's family or the young person themselves may not make this easy.

3.1.5 Some homes have well established procedures for admission and staff training sessions which provide good coverage of what is involved. In others, the quality of admission depends largely on the initiative of the member of staff on duty, with perhaps little or no training to assist her or him. This seems an inadequate way to establish a sound basis for care of any kind. A sensitively prepared admission procedure is required; this should be fully understood by all staff and by field workers and others having regular contact with the home. The procedure should be regularly reviewed and young people who have been admitted to the home should be involved in contributing to the review of the procedure since their experience will provide most useful insights. Admission for short periods, including respite care, should be handled with equal sensitivity and attention to detail.

3.1.6   The admission procedure should include discussion of the statement of rights and responsibilities which, as recommended in section II of this Chapter, should be issued on or before admission to every young person.

> **Recommendation 8: Local authority and agency managers should ensure that a comprehensive admission procedure has been drawn up for each home, that all care staff are trained in the procedure, and that it is known to field staff and others with regular professional contact with the home. The procedure should be reviewed at least annually, and the young people in the home should be assisted to contribute to this review.**

Maintaining Personal Identity

3.1.7   Young people in residential care should be able to maintain and, in many cases, recover a sense of their own identity as a person of worth. Their experiences, their circumstances or their own behaviour may for many have undermined this basic human need for positive recognition. It is a challenging part of the residential care worker's task to help the young person with these difficulties, but this is an area in which training seems frequently inadequate at present. The task will be assisted or hindered by the general approach to matters of identity and privacy in the home or school.

3.1.8   Young people in residential homes and schools are in some ways exposed to adult observation, comment and expectations somewhat exceeding those experienced by young people in their own family homes. They can find it difficult to "get away from being in a home for just an hour". For most people "home" is a place of individual privacy, as well as of belonging. Some children's homes in Scotland recognise this very sensitively, but for others it seems necessary to emphasise that a children's home is a place where people live. Nowadays it is unlikely to be the staff's home, but it is still the children's home, and the degree of privacy and dignity it affords them is important.

3.1.9   There are some single rooms in today's children's homes, but there are also many which are shared. It can be argued that no child should be expected to share a room with a complete stranger. Sometimes young people do want to share a room with another, and this can reduce the sense of loneliness which many young people in residential care feel. Each young person or child needs both companionship and privacy at different times.

3.1.10   Some bedrooms in Scottish children's homes are poorly furnished and drab, particularly in units where children do not stay very long. There are some good examples of colourful rooms, personalised with posters and possessions. All bedrooms should have wardrobes, a chest of drawers and mirrors. Young people must have opportunities to imprint their own identity on things. Even in secure accommodation, it should be possible to provide some means of reflecting the character of the inhabitants. Leaving clothes and belongings in piles on the floor for the lack of anywhere else to put them can only provoke despair; regrettably it has been the only course available to young people in some units. Replacement programmes should include more appropriate bedroom accommodation as well as bed-sitting rooms and small flats.

3.1.11   Young people feel very strongly that they are entitled to have some control over the access to their own rooms. In some homes residents take great pride in their rooms and their appearance. Sadly, in others, the degree of stealing is such that birthday presents have a life of 2 or 3 days. It is advisable to consider doors that can always be opened from the inside, but only lockable from the outside. Young people should have keys, even though they may lose them; possession of your own key is a sign of, as well as a means to, real security. Many children will continue to share rooms and so some other arrangement must be made for secure storage over which they have control; for instance, a lockable drawer or cupboard.

3.1.12 It is important that privacy is preserved for visitors and for personal discussions with staff. Taking relatives to a well maintained single bedroom may ensure privacy but is not always possible. In any event it is inappropriate to meet all visitors in a bedroom and some other ground floor provision is necessary in addition to the public rooms.

3.1.13 Everyone is generally entitled to send and receive private mail; everyone is generally entitled to make and receive telephone calls in private in their own home; young people and children in residential care should be similarly entitled to these things. Homes, of course, need appropriate rules to control the duration, frequency and distance of telephone calls and may need the technology to bar certain types of calls, or frequency of calls.

3.1.14 All this applies equally to children and young people with complex special needs. Additionally, they require accommodation that facilitates their care, safety and independence; as for example through the provision of adapted toilets and showers and access to all relevant parts of the building. Their need for assistance with personal care should be carried out ensuring the dignity of, and privacy for, the children.

> **Recommendations 9: Where locks are fitted to bedroom doors these should only be lockable from the outside and always be able to be opened from the inside. (Except for secure accommodation). Where bedrooms are shared, each young person or child should have a lockable cupboard or drawer. Young people and children should be able to make and receive telephone calls in private.**

> **Recommendation 10: In homes and residential schools providing care for children and young people with complex social and educational needs accommodation should be designed, or adapted, to facilitate high quality care practices and access.**

Young People Who Have Been Sexually Abused

3.1.15 The heightened awareness of sexual abuse has appropriately resulted in increased sensitivity to this issue. An increasing number of young people and children reveal that they have been abused and inevitably a proportion has to come into care, either for the protection of the young people, or because of the ensuing family crises. In some units a high number of young people have been physically, sexually or emotionally abused; sometimes this may be known at the time of reception into care, but in other cases once the young person has settled in, and has found someone to trust, she or he tells the staff member about the abuse. Although knowledge from research is still at an early stage and inconclusive, there is a growing appreciation that the effects of sexual abuse on young people and children are painful and rarely straightforward. The effects may manifest themselves in disturbing ways.

3.1.16 Young people who have been abused are inevitably deeply troubled and need help to make sense of what has happened in the context of their whole lives. Sometimes confusion and distress leads to behaviour which can be disruptive to other residents, and present staff with complex difficulties requiring sensitive handling. For instance; they may inflict injuries on themselves; their poor regard for themselves may result in poor hygiene; they may lose, or fail to develop, a clear sense of appropriate boundaries for sexual behaviour; they may develop fears of different people or situations; and sometimes they may put themselves, and others, at risk by introducing sexual under-tones to fleeting and superficial contacts.

3.1.17 Caring for young people who have been sexually abused presents considerable challenges to residential staff. The task is often stressful and demanding. Many, and not solely those who are not professionally qualified, are ill-equipped to respond adequately. Knowledge of the effects of abuse is developing but the subject remains characterised by uncertainty. Residential staff require training and careful support to ensure that sensitive and appropriate responses to children are promoted. They need regular opportunities to keep up with developments in knowledge and practice. Effective supervision and management are essential to assist staff to plan and undertake this work.

3.1.18   These changed demands on residential staff are reflected in recommendations on staffing and training in Chapter 4.

Young People Who Abuse Others.

3.1.19   The research literature points to the fact that many people who become convicted child sexual abusers start their "career" in sexual offending in adolescence, or even earlier. Most young people in children's homes never have and never will abuse others. However, it is clear that some do. The fact that some young people in residential care present a risk to other young people in homes and schools has been highlighted by English studies, and it was clear from several submissions, and from visits, that staff in Scottish children's homes are confronting similar problems. More research to establish the position clearly is required.

3.1.20   Some young people and children do enter into exploitative relationships and abuse others; some do so as a means of acting out and dealing with their own abuse. It is clear, however, that not all victims of abuse demonstrate sexually abusive behaviour to others. It is wrong to consider that many of those who have been abused themselves as children necessarily go on to abuse others. It may also be wrong to consider that many of those who sexually abuse children have themselves been abused. Early findings from a research study commissioned by the Scottish Office indicate that perhaps only a small proportion of adult sexual abusers have themselves been victims of abuse.[4]

3.1.21   It is impossible to really judge whether there is now more sexual abuse than there was in the past, or whether, as seems likely, what has happened is that abuse which was previously hidden has been uncovered, and clearly condemned. Whatever the case, the management of this disturbing behaviour places new and heavy demands on residential staff, who must strive to balance the very different needs of individual children, some of whom have been abused and others who have been abusing. Young people and children who have been abused must be protected from further abuse and, of course, all children placed in residential provision are entitled to protection. Consequently consideration may need to be given to separating young people known to abuse others, from more vulnerable children. Separation in specialist provision will not always be realistic, however, because of the numbers involved, the difficulty in identifying young people who abuse others, and the danger that victims themselves may becomes abusers. It may not be desirable if it risks stigmatisation and isolation which may trap a young person into patterns of anti-social behaviour.

3.1.22   Where young people who have been abused and young people known to have abused others have to be placed in the same residential unit, there must be careful assessment of the risks, agreed protection plans and appropriate levels of surveillance. Work will also require to be undertaken to enable the young person to accept responsibility for the behaviour and learn more appropriate ways of relating to others. This has implications for agencies placement policies, staffing levels, training and supervision and requires access to external expert consultancy.

> *Recommendation 11: The Social Work Services Inspectorate, after consultation, should issue practice guidance on providing residential care for young people and children who have been abused and those who abuse others.*

Ethnic Minorities

3.1.23   The individual needs of young people and children from ethnic minorities in Scotland's children's homes merit special consideration. Being alone can often compound the vulnerability that exists because of race, ethnic origin or colour. This is an area in which training for both managers and staff is generally inadequate under current arrangements.

---

[4] "Effective Management of Child Sexual Abuse in Scotland".
Dr Dobash, Dr Carnie, L Waterhouse, University of Edinburgh/University of Wales, 1992.

3.1.24   Organisations must pay attention to a young person's racial, cultural, religious and linguistic needs. This should automatically be a part of the due heed to be given to every child's emotional development. With the best will in the world, however, most white staff are not equipped to provide adequate support because they lack training and guidance. If there are language difficulties, perhaps with parents, then arrangements for interpreting must be made. It is important that educational and other material available should be of a kind which helps to provide positive images of members of ethnic minority communities. Literature regarding the purpose and procedures of the home should be available in the appropriate ethnic languages.

3.1.25   Racial harassment is sadly a feature in Scottish society today and constitutes a serious problem. It is imperative that staff and agencies are alert to it and receive appropriate training.

> **Recommendation 12: In-service training for residential child care staff should include racial awareness training. Residential staff and managers should have training in anti-discriminatory practice.**

Young People And Children with Disabilities

3.1.26   In Scotland there are 335 children in care who have disabilities of whom 168 are in residential homes, hospitals, or residential schools.

3.1.27   Many children with disabilities are cared for away from home on a short-term basis as part of a planned programme of respite care; the numbers would appear to be smaller than those who may require such care. There is a demand for flexible short-term care which provides: -

a local service, where the child can continue to attend school as if he or she were living at home;

good quality child care in which parents have confidence, which ensures that the young person is treated first as an individual and where provision is made for special needs arising from his or her disabilities;

care in partnership with parents as part of their network of support with, so far as possible, parents choosing patterns of use; and

continuation of the special programmes drawn up to promote the development of the individual.

A small number of families might benefit from respite for the whole family, designed to meet the different needs of members of a family. This can be appropriate for some families with a child with a life-threatening condition, or with serious episodes of critical illness which affect the whole family. Some families seek such respite in children's hospices.

3.1.28   There is also a need for longer term residential care for some children who have substantial medical, para-medical and nursing needs. Such children should be placed in a non-hospital setting with an input from child health services where required.

3.1.29   Residential and respite care, with or without education, for young people with disabilities should be governed by the same principles that underpin all good residential child care. The unit should be small, homely, accommodating 6-8 children, integrated within the community, readily accessible, positively involving parents and providing a caring, stimulating and therapeutic environment. Children with disabilities should have access to all the accommodation and have the same rights to privacy as any other child. For example, the management of incontinence or other personal care needs necessitates suitable bathroom accommodation which offers space, privacy, sufficient hot water and which is conveniently located near other living areas.

3.1.30   There are some good examples of provision for young people with disabilities by both local authorities and voluntary organisations in Scotland. But they are too few in number and some are inadequately adapted. It is estimated that around 70 children with multiple special needs are living in long-stay hospital care. Whilst a considerable effort has been made to reduce numbers to this level, it is important that efforts to provide residential care in other settings are continued. A greater range of services is required to meet the diversity of special needs, and particularly for those children with disturbed or disturbing behaviour highly specialised multi-disciplinary provision may be required.

3.1.31 Children with disabilities living in residential care are particularly vulnerable. Those who lack mobility or have learning and communication difficulties, or both, are very dependant upon staff. For this group, agencies and staff must be especially aware of their responsibilities and ensure that high quality care and provision to meet their special needs are in place. Staff should be active members of multi-disciplinary teams, responsible for each individual young person.

> *Recommendation 13: Children with disabilities who require substitute home care but not treatment should be cared for in specialised residential or family provision and not in hospitals. Local authorities and health boards should develop their plans for the discharge of children in long-stay hospitals. The Scottish Office should consider an appropriate target date for the discharge of all children in long-stay hospitals who do not require to be there.*

Preparation For Adulthood

3.1.32 All care is in part a preparation for adult life. Young people in residential care need to have the opportunity to practice making choices in respect of small decisions in their lives. It is therefore crucial that they are able, as appropriate to their age and development, to choose clothing, toiletries, pictures for their walls, colour schemes for their rooms where possible and to participate in food shopping and planning menus and activities. The encouragement to undertake these and to provide support in making mistakes where necessary, is an important preparation for their future independence.

3.1.33 There are several good examples of "training flats" within residential units, and of "satellite houses" - tenancies near to residential units, through which ex-residents can maintain support links. Many residential staff are highly skilled in this area of work. Several homes have adapted their accommodation imaginatively in order to provide a separate and semi-independent unit. They and their agencies are confident about the purpose and value of the work they are doing in this area and that is reflected in the quality of much of what is done. The young people in most of the independent units appear to enjoy the experiences and opportunities open to them. Generally they appear to have a clear sense of the supports available to them and of their own responsibilities.

3.1.34 Preparation for adulthood is not simply "preparation for independence". The bases for many adult competencies are established when a child is quite young and are a part of residential care no matter how short a time a child spends in a home. The disadvantageous effects of failing to provide these opportunities is well known and documented and all homes need to give attention to how they can offer as many decisions as possible to young people in their care.

3.1.35 The ways of assisting young people to independence range from involving them in domestic tasks to presenting possible housing and support options to a prospective care leaver, and encouraging choices. The inhibiting factors for staff in developing this area, as fully as they might, are lack of time, their frequent lack of training (discussed in Chapter 4) and organisational constraints around the way basic care provision is made (discussed in section III of this chapter).

Leaving Care And Afterwards

3.1.36 Young people may leave a home because their circumstances have changed; for example, an appropriate family place has been found; their behaviour has changed; or they are ready to live more independently. Whatever the reason and circumstances their leaving needs to be prepared for and sensitively handled, as it is another important transition in what for many is a life of difficult changes.

3.1.37   Homes with a reasonably stable group of residents, and a predictable set of expectations, can prepare young people and children well for moving on. Residential staff can and often do play an important part in easing the transition period and maintaining contact with the young person wherever they have moved to. In many homes, however, it is difficult to find the time to undertake this work effectively. Key workers regularly express the wish to retain contact with young people after they leave care. Often the key worker has become very important to the young person and may be the only person of real continuing significance in their life. Staff often feel unable to follow through on work with these young people because of their more immediate care responsibilities. As a consequence, some staff follow up young people in their own time. Since it is a primary objective of residential child care to help young people make good relationships, careful thought needs to be given to ways in which these relationships can be preserved when they leave care. Young people often revisit their residential unit after leaving, and sometimes they receive substantial support from the unit. Some adults (of all ages) revisit, perhaps when a home is due for closure, and these emotional events need sensitive handling.

3.1.38   Homes which are integrated at a local level as part of a range of resources find it easier to adapt staff roles flexibly so that members can sometimes work with children, young people and their families before they come into care, as well as helping to support young people after they have left. There are a number of good examples of this kind of provision in Scotland.

3.1.39   When young people are leaving care in order to live independently, the timing of this move and the availability of continuing support are crucial. By and large young people are not able to be fully independent at the age of 16. For most people parental support, however intermittent, carries on into their twenties. Young people and children in care also need this continuing support but often are not able to get it.

3.1.40   There was a tendency for young people to move out of residential care as soon as they possibly could, often as soon as they reached 16. With changes in the regulations covering benefit entitlements several local authorities in Scotland have adapted their policies and practices to provide care and support for longer periods of a young person's life.

3.1.41   Support and accommodation are linked central elements of a successful move away from care. To this end some social work departments have been able to establish close links with housing departments and housing associations, and also with those voluntary organisations which provide support in a variety of forms. Several have well organised teams providing supported accommodation developed with imagination, skill and close working with colleagues. These schemes include landladies who provide support, shared flats and neighbourhood support schemes. Voluntary organisations may play an important part; for example one successful scheme has catered specifically for young women who have been sexually abused; another example of good practice is a scheme where young people with profound learning difficulties are settled into a community home during the latter stages of school, and are eased into a more appropriate adult lifestyle.

3.1.42   In many areas, however, there is no supported accommodation scheme and insufficient staff resources to deploy in setting one up. Those schemes in operation are unable to meet the demand placed on them and a significant increase in the amount of supported accommodation for young people from care is needed including those with extra needs due to disabilities.

3.1.43   The Child Care Law Review[5] made a number of recommendations in respect of young people leaving care and the need for after-care support. The recommendations were that;

> "local authorities should be under a duty to advise and assist children and young people during any period they spend in care, in order to prepare them for future life when they leave care (No 23);"

[5] "Care Management Assessment, Practitioners Guide", SSI and SWSG HMSO, 1991.

"local authorities should have a duty to provide advice and assistance to any young person over minimum school leaving age who has spent a significant part of their life in care since attaining age 12 whenever that young person requests it and when their needs, in the opinion of the local authority, require it. Where provided, such assistance should be available until the young person attains age 21 (No 24); and"

"Every local authority should be required to establish a range of services to offer young people who have been in care (No 25)."

Local Authorities have already begun to implement the spirit of these recommendations, but more comprehensive provision is required.

> **Recommendation 14: The recommendations of the Child Care Law Review (Recommendations 23-25) which are concerned to extend the local authorities after-care responsibilities should be implemented as soon as resources allow.**

Assessing Outcomes

3.1.44   Local authorities and other agencies assess individual needs in some cases with great care and in considerable detail. Assessment guides and proformas have been developed from a number of different theoretical perspectives. For many young people and children admitted into residential care, with or without education, the approach to assessment is, however, rather unsystematic. This raises problems firstly, in ensuring that all the individual developmental needs of the young person or child are identified and met and secondly, in evaluating the outcomes of the care which is provided. In addition to the problems for individuals this frequent lack of a systematic approach has led to considerable difficulty in more generally evaluating the benefits of different forms of care. The guidance on Care Management and Assessment (HMSO 1991)[5] has particular relevance for the assessment of children who require a co-ordinated care plan such as children with disabilities.

3.1.45   The report of an independent working party established by the Department of Health on Child Care Outcomes was published at the end of last year.[6] This provides a series of six schedules designed to monitor children's progress up to 18 years, and to regularly review the quality of care they receive and the extent to which the everyday tasks of parenting are being adequately carried out. The forms are intended to be used in the first instance at an initial review to set a base line standard of care for assessed need, and thereafter at regular review intervals. The packs consisting of Facts Sheets, Review and Planning Forms, and Assessment and Action Records for children of different ages, are intended for practical use. The records are designed to direct attention to aspects of development which are often overlooked and to help social workers, parents, foster carers and residential staff to ensure a consistency of care in areas that give rise to concern. They should also make it possible for serious deficiencies in the care provided to be picked up more quickly.

3.1.46   The scheme has been piloted in five authorities in England and is now being implemented and carefully monitored by a research team based at the University of Bristol. Initial findings showed that the approach was well accepted by social workers and managers and resulted in some significant improvements in practice. Scottish authorities had some earlier involvement in the work leading up to the project. The report and packs of schedules have already been sent to Directors of Social Work in Scotland who may wish to consider pilot projects.

3.1.47   Residential care staff are in a good position to pilot the use of these new tools and they would certainly assist with the residential care task. It would also be of benefit for residential care staff to be in the forefront of this professional development. It is also very important to establish better information about the outcomes of placements in residential homes with and without education. For these reasons it is recommended that local authorities and other agencies consider piloting the new schedules in residential homes and schools. Education departments have their own assessment and action records which might also be considered for wider use in residential care. There is considerable scope in this area for collaborative developments.

[5] "Review of Child Care Law in Scotland" The Scottish Office, HMSO, Edinburgh 1990.

[6] Parker, Roy et al (Ed) 1991 Assessing Outcomes in Child Care, London, HMSO

Recommendation 15: The Social Work Services Inspectorate should evaluate Looking After Children: Assessing Outcomes in Child Care and issue practice guidance.

II. RIGHTS

> Young people, children and their parents should be given a clear statement of their rights
> and responsibilities. They should have a confidential means of making complaints. They
> should be involved in decisions affecting them and the running of the home. Their rights
> should be consistently respected.

3.2.1   Young people and children in residential care are amongst the most vulnerable in society and
special attention must be given to protecting their rights. Their lives are very largely determined
by decisions made by others and perhaps their most important right is to have those decisions
made with care. It is therefore important to ensure that language and other communication skills
are available to these children who have problems with language.

Statements Of Rights And Responsibilities

3.2.2   The quality of staff and the quality of staff training is fundamental to promoting and protecting
the rights of young people and children in residential care.

3.2.3   Two particular rights are under the greatest threat from the pressures of modern society, and under
particular threat of being neglected for young people and children in residential care. They are,
firstly;

   – a child has a right to her or his childhood,
     a young person a right to her or his youth;

and secondly;

   – young people and children have a right to have all decisions about them made with the
     greatest care.

3.2.4   These rights can be clearly stated but not easily measured. They depend to a large extent on the
quality and training of staff which is considered further in Chapter 4.

3.2.5   Several agencies have adopted statements or "Charters" of rights for young people and children
in care. Many have based theirs on the "Who Cares" Charter[7] which has served as a good model.
Some agencies have handbooks providing a range of important information including a statement
of rights, and those which have been produced in close collaboration with young people in care,
or who have been in care, are particularly useful. Many homes and most young people and
children in care do not have a statement of their rights and responsibilities. That individuals have
intellectual disabilities is no reason for not having such a statement. It is important to achieve
consistent good practice for every agency and home.

3.2.6   Statements ought to include information about responsibilities as well as rights since otherwise
young people are only being given half the picture. It is important that they should know where
they stand overall, and that means that they must be informed clearly about their responsibilities
as well as their rights. The "Who Cares" charter is a useful national contribution, but it lacks a
statement of responsibilities.

3.2.7   Statements of rights and responsibilities should be developed by the agencies responsible for
ensuring they are adhered to in daily practice. After their development statements should be
adopted in a purposeful way to increase commitment to meeting the obligations they imply, and
they should be regularly reviewed. A central initiative or promulgation of a charter of rights for
young people in residential care would detract from this requirement to obtain full agency
commitment to the statements. The government has ratified the UN Convention on The Rights
Of The Child and this provides a general framework within which agencies can develop their own
statements and charters. There are several good models already in use in Scotland to draw upon.

---

[7] Charter of Rights for Young People in Care, "Who Cares", Scotland 1986.

3.2.8 Every young person or child in residential care should have a copy of a statement of rights and responsibilities - preferably before they are admitted. The statement should cover key points in relation to the eight principles considered in this chapter.

3.2.9 A particular right, which is rarely covered in statements or procedures is the right to consult a general practitioner, and to be able to do so without informing care staff or others, and without having to explain the reason for the consultation. This right should be clearly spelled out for young people and children in residential care.

> **Recommendation 16: All agencies involved in residential child care should prepare a statement of rights and responsibilities of young people and children in care. This should cover key points in relation to the eight principles outlined in this report, and include their rights to consult a general practitioner, and to complain confidentially; it should also outline their responsibilities in relation to behaviour and the specific rules of the home. Before (or at the latest on) admission to a home every young person or child should be given a copy of this statement. Such statements should be available in other language forms (including Braille) when necessary.**

Complaints

3.2.10 Local social work authorities and organisations with which they contract services are now obliged to have formal complaints procedures, and to publish details of them. In 1991 the Social Work Services Group issued guidance on complaints procedures, including guidance regarding residential child care. Local authorities have responded speedily in setting up complaints procedures.

3.2.11 Young people and children in care should understand and have ready access to these procedures. They are often unwilling to raise complaints because they do not wish to see any individual blamed, or because they do not believe the complaint will be fairly dealt with, or because they do not expect a good standard of care. The complaints procedure is no easy solution to problems which exist, but it is important that agencies should promote the schemes which they have. It is also important that the complaints should be dealt with independently of the home and its managers.

3.2.12 Young people need to be able to make their complaints in confidence, and to make them to someone independent from the residential home. Some agencies have issued telephone numbers or contact cards to which confidential calls can be made. Childline offers an extremely important service in this regard. Young people and children in residential care should be able to raise complaints entirely confidentially to someone who is not involved in the management of the home. Managers will always have to deal with a number of complaints, but they are under a range of different pressures, some of which may militate against thorough investigation and resolution of complaints. They, as well as the young people, should have the capacity to refer particular complaints on to a more independent agent. Additional arrangements should be made to monitor the quality of provision for children and young people who are not able to complain on their own behalf, due to communication or language differences.

3.2.13 Complaints of physical or sexual abuse by staff are especially difficult to raise. Where the allegations are clearly directed at one person some agencies immediately suspend the staff member accused and conduct an investigation. This is not always appropriate, and can lead to staff demoralisation and ineffectiveness if it is an automatic response. It is more important that the allegation should be clearly taken seriously, and thoroughly investigated by an independent person than that there should necessarily be any immediate action regarding staff members. The police should be informed whenever there is reasonable cause to believe that a child may have been the victim of abuse; they can then determine how to conduct any subsequent investigation, and judge how extensive it should be. Where appropriate the police will, after making an initial assessment, consult with other agencies.

3.2.14 Strengthening the independence of the person responsible for investigation of complaints is in the interests of staff, as well as of young people; such independence should be a requirement of local procedures. Local authorities and other agencies will need to tackle this requirement in different ways and should establish appropriate local liaison arrangements.

3.2.15 The use of formal complaints procedures is bound to remain very limited. In any field formal complaints are a very small percentage of total complaints and faults. Informal complaints, therefore, need to be carefully listened to and passed on to the person who has the authority to deal with it. Allegations of physical or sexual abuse by staff, whether made as formal complaints or not, should always be handled by staff outwith the home. They should not be handled by the officer-in-charge. This is because such a procedure would enable matters to be covered over too easily, whether intentionally or not.

> *Recommendation 17: All young people and children in residential care should be able to make a confidential complaint without the knowledge of the staff of the home. Parents of young people and children in residential care should similarly be able to make a complaint in confidence.*

> *Recommendation 18: Complaints, allegations, or suspicions of physical or sexual abuse of young people or children in residential care, should always be referred to managers, or appointed agents, outwith the home and its management; they should, in every instance where there is reasonable cause to believe that a child may have been the victim of abuse, inform the police. A record should be kept of any allegations made.*

Involvement In Decisions

3.2.16 Neither having a statement of rights nor the ability to complain in confidence is the heart of the matter. Young people do not generally want to complain; what they do invariably want is to be involved in decisions.

3.2.17 Some residential homes provide good examples of the involvement of young people and children in decisions. Through discussion with individuals, and through paying careful attention to young people's meetings, these homes involve young people and children in decisions about the running of the home as well as about their own situations.

3.2.18 A great many young people and children, however, do not feel involved in decisions, either about their own lives, or about the home in which they live. Most young people and children feel completely helpless, confused and powerless at the time they are received into care and, for too many, this feeling tends to be compounded by their experiences thereafter. Young people are, for instance, too seldom given the opportunity to consider or say whether they would prefer residential care, or another kind of care. If options are well expressed most children and young people with learning difficulties are also perfectly capable of making sensible choices. Only in exceptional circumstances should others make decisions for them, and in such cases, family members or other interested friends should be consulted first.

3.2.19 Implementation of recommendation 19 of the Child Care Law Review would assist. It states that

> *"Children aged 12 and over should have a statutory right of attendance at case reviews; requests from younger children to attend should be considered in the light of their age and capacity to understand; and care authorities should be required to prepare children and young persons for such attendance".*

3.2.20 But involvement will be meaningless if the review is not carefully prepared and properly run, and its decisions not made with care. If decisions about young people and children in residential homes are always to meet the test of being made with care, then two matters need attention. The first is the training of residential child care staff, which frequently seems inadequate for the complex and demanding tasks they face.

3.2.21   The second is the care with which statutory child care reviews (which are required to be held regularly to consider the progress, circumstances and plans for the young person or child) are arranged, prepared and conducted. Reviews of young people in residential care are generally more timeous than other reviews, and in some respects are easier to prepare and conduct. Review meetings are often quite large, and are inevitably daunting occasions for young people and children, no matter how well-prepared. If they are at all uncertain about the purpose and nature of the review, then the value of their, and indeed other people's involvement, will be much diminished.

3.2.22   Young people need to be assisted to be active participants in reviews. They must have access to reports and full information on who else is attending and why. Reviews are about the young person or child involved and she or he is likely to have the most anxieties about its content and timing. Too often, however, the young person is not consulted about the timing or, when it occurs, about postponement. They should be given clearer rights in the process. This is true also in respect of their parents. These are matters of good practice and procedure rather than requiring central regulation. Local procedures could include provision that statutory child care reviews should not be postponed or cancelled without prior discussion with the young person or child involved. Where a review had not been arranged within the statutory period a young person, child or their parents could have a procedural right to require that one be arranged within four weeks of their requiring it. Consideration should be given to the need for representation in special cases separate from parents, for children who have communication problems which do not allow them to participate.

> **Recommendation 19: All young people and children in residential care should have the right to consider, with other young people and children, issues regarding the running of their home and to make suggestions and recommendations. Local authorities should consider instituting local procedural rights for young people and their parents to the effect that no review should be postponed without consulting them, and that they should be able to require that an overdue review be called.**

Advocacy

3.2.23   A child has a right to her or his childhood; a young person a right to her or his youth. They must not, therefore, be given all the responsibilities of adulthood, and at times, should be able to call on someone to act as their advocate.

3.2.24   The law in Scotland already recognises a number of different possibilities for advocacy depending on the circumstances of the young person. In considering the need for a Child Welfare Commission in Scotland, the Child Care Law Review pointed out the difficulties of keeping sight of the overall welfare of a young person, even where the various agencies are all fulfilling their separate functions adequately. Often the difficulty is not that young people and children do not have enough rights, but that staff and parents do not have enough information to help them exercise their rights.

3.2.25   Whatever may develop in the future, there is an immediate need to ensure that all those involved in working with young people and children in residential care have a good knowledge of the young people's rights in statutory proceedings and other matters, including rights within local procedures and benefit entitlements. Some residential care staff are extremely well informed; many are not and lack training in this area. Children and young people with Record of Needs may have a "Named Person" who takes an interest in matters related to the recording process.

3.2.26   There is already one post of Children's Rights Officer in one Scottish authority and other authorities have similar posts with different titles. The established Children's' Rights Officer is mainly concerned with two stages of the complaints procedure; firstly, notification of a complaint and secondly, advocacy and support. Most complaints are settled without the need to move on to the second stage, but if this proves necessary, the Children's Rights Officer is able to support and represent the child until a satisfactory conclusion is reached.

3.2.27 This specialist approach has much to offer, and is supported by "Who Cares". A similar post in Leicestershire was instrumental in uncovering problems there. Children's Rights Officers in social work departments can provide a useful background for children's rights and promote good practice in residential child care. They also provide an appropriate way of handling the vast majority of complaints and concerns.

3.2.28 However, they cannot be considered to be independent of the department. It has been suggested that rights officers could be employed by voluntary organisations and contracted with social work departments, thus making them independent of management. Against this it has been argued that the voluntary organisation's dependence on grant also reduces independence, and that an officer employed by the authority is likely to wield more influence internally.

3.2.29 There is no single correct or simple solution to providing appropriate advocacy for young people in residential care. All staff working with young people have responsibilities to act as their advocates in some circumstances. Specialist posts can be of benefit in themselves, and in heightening the awareness of others. Local authorities should consider increasing the number of such posts. Some authorities, and agencies, are not large enough to support a full-time specialist post, but they could consider either joining with others, or making part-time appointments. Some voluntary organisations have created advocacy services for people with disabilities who are less able to represent themselves. Such services should be considered and available for some children in care who have disabilities, particularly when they are approaching adulthood.

3.2.30 Though they may serve the majority of more general concerns well, these arrangements may not deal with the most serious concerns, or the situations where young people are most vulnerable. A separate independent children's advocacy service would, however, be difficult to establish. Moreover children need local access to assistance, which would be difficult to sustain on a national basis. The arrangements for complaints and the general functioning of homes and schools should be kept under review by those in the most senior positions including councillors and chief officers.

3.2.31 It is essential that young people, children and their parents should have a clear route to having complaints considered independently from the home and its managers. In the majority of cases they will not wish to follow that route, and will prefer a very quick and straightforward resolution of their grievance, at a very local level. But their access to independent assessment of serious complaints must never be blocked. This requires that each and any professional adult in contact with a young person or child must be prepared to act in part as their advocate.

"Who Cares"

3.2.32 "Who Cares" is the national organisation of young people and children in care. Some of its central costs are funded by the Scottish Office and the costs of some local groups and staff are funded by local authorities.

3.2.33 Effective consumer groups, like "Who Cares", are not easy to establish or maintain. "Who Cares" faces the additional organisational difficulties of the age of the group they represent, and the fact that their members keep growing up and moving on. The organisation has nonetheless established itself as an effective voice, both nationally, and in those regions where it is active and supported. Young people and children who have contact with "Who Cares" clearly value this.

3.2.34 That is because "Who Cares" reduces their sense of powerlessness, because they can see occasional results of their advocacy and because it provides opportunities to share their experience and feelings about being in care. For many the motivation of their involvement is clearly to improve the quality of care experienced by others.

3.2.35   "Who Cares" contributed valuably to the work of this review. Its members provided important insights to their experience of care and to how care could be improved. All of "Who Cares" presentations and arguments had been maturely and carefully considered.

> **Recommendations 20: Each local authority should consider supporting the development of "Who Cares" appropriate for its Region, and should ensure that all those in care can have access to it. The Scottish Office should consider the continued funding of "Who Cares" nationally, subject to a review every three years.**

III. GOOD BASIC CARE

Young people and children in residential care with or without education should be given a high standard of personal care. They should be offered new, varied and positive experiences of life, and should be included in the wider community.

Buildings

3.3.1   Many of the buildings used in Scotland today as residential homes for young people and children are inappropriate and are not suited to the job. Some of these homes should be closed and replaced. Many were closed without being replaced during the dramatic drop in the numbers of children in care during the 1980s, but this will prove less possible over the next few years.

3.3.2   The main problem is the size of some homes. Many are too big to provide the necessary sense of individual care and belonging. Over a quarter of "homes" have more than 20 beds. Larger homes allow economies of scale in staffing and in the organisation of certain activities; but it is much more important that young people should get personalised attention, and, where possible, that leisure and recreation activities take place in the community. There is no optimum size of home; much depends on its functions and objectives and the resulting staffing requirements. It is vital that young people should not feel intimidated, alienated or de-personalised by the size of the home; if they are, then the economies of staffing achieved by larger homes will be more than off-set by failures in effectiveness. In smaller homes there is more individual care; and there should be less bullying, and fewer problems of control, where the numbers are smaller. As the Convention of Scottish Local Authorities and the Association of Directors of Social Work have stated, smaller units in smaller buildings are likely to be more manageable, and more effective in meeting the needs of most young people. An inevitable consequence of moving to smaller units is the increase in staff which will be required.

3.3.3   The age of the buildings is not necessarily a significant factor in the quality of home. The important issue is not age, but how well fitted the building is for its purpose. Large mansions are rarely able to offer an appropriate atmosphere, or the right layout, no matter how carefully they are divided into internal units.

3.3.4   Some homes are inappropriately located. Choice of location is a complex issue for which there are no easy answers. Some homes that are rather isolated can offer a good deal of warmth and care and, so long as they are not too big, can provide opportunities for integration in ways appropriate for their young people. Some others located within communities can encounter great problems in seeking to establish good local relationships for the young people to draw on. Sometimes a home can become a scapegoat, and be blamed for all the vandalism and anti-social behaviour that takes place. In extreme but rare cases, in the face of local hostility it can become necessary to close the home. Generally, homes need to be well served by public transport, to be in or near to a community to which they can belong, and to have access to schools and to leisure facilities. Smaller homes in ordinary houses are likely to have fewer problems of local acceptance than purpose built homes easily identified for what they are. Some homes have established good links with their neighbours and much credit is due to officers-in-charge, and their staff, for the way in which this has been done. Some authorities have encountered strong local objection to the establishment of new, smaller homes. There is no evidence of a detrimental effect on property values, local youth relationships or behaviour and these objections are unjustified.

3.3.5   The maintenance of the fabric of some homes, particularly in the local authorities' own provision, has been badly neglected. Some good local authority homes are in excellent condition, but many are not. For some a proper inspection, rather than this review's inevitably briefer visits, may well lead to recommendations for closure. For all homes, the look and feel of the building are significant factors in setting the atmosphere and general approach. The whole question of respect for the residents has to be reflected in the care of their building. No one can learn respect for themselves or others who is not first shown it, and the external appearance, the gardens, and the notices are all part of the care provided. Young people in residential care have to be helped to feel valued and unpainted walls, broken doors, torn curtains and damaged furniture do nothing to help.

3.3.6 Difficulties arise because repairs are not completed promptly. In some cases minor repairs to locks, doors or cupboards can take 6 weeks or more. Sometimes remedial work is undertaken quickly but a painter has not come to finish it off for several weeks. Homes in the voluntary and private sectors are mainly in better condition. This may partly be because they do not have the same bureaucratic processes to go through. Repairs in the private and voluntary homes seem to be generally speedily completed, as in the few local authority homes with devolved budgets. It is a simple truth that if you sustain good fabric, and complete repairs with dispatch, it is more likely the young people will maintain it that way.

3.3.7 Young people with disabilities who use a variety of equipment and wheelchairs require sufficient space to store and to use them effectively. If space is too limited, equipment can sometimes be abandoned, creating more dependency on staff and reducing the child's opportunities for control of their own abilities. The internal fabric and furniture can become scratched and splintered creating a shabby environment for all living in the home or school. The physical environment needs to be adapted to minimise the effects of disability by providing the necessary equipment and facilities without detracting from the appearance of an ordinary homely setting.

3.3.8 There are essentially two requirements for improving the physical provision - acceleration of replacement programmes and better maintenance.

3.3.9 Estimates of the cost of a replacement programme vary enormously and cannot be accurately estimated. Some authorities are establishing new systems for asset management and these welcome initiatives are likely to provide better information as well as better management. The Scottish Office's removal of the requirement for project approval is entirely appropriate in emphasising local authorities' own responsibilities in these areas. However, better central information, on capital assets and future likely patterns, is also required if the overall programme and policies are to be effectively monitored. Replacement programmes which have started need to be accelerated if a good quality of care is to be provided. To achieve this greater priority will require to be given by both central and local government to the capital needs in this area. In time, the programme will realise capital assets as the sites and buildings of unsuitable old homes are sold off.

3.3.10 **Better maintenance** of the fabric of the building and the furniture might well be achieved by devolving more authority for these matters to the officer-in-charge (see Chapter 5 on management issues). This would enable more of them to achieve what is commonly achieved in the independent homes, i.e. repairs attended to within 24 hours. Clear recognition of the fact that young people are in the care of the authority as a whole and not just of the Social Work Department will also assist; in important respects a child's experience of care may be determined by the Works Department. Local authorities should set good standards for the maintenance, repair and general furbishment of children's homes provided by themselves or any agency, and local Inspection Units should monitor and report on the achievement of these standards.

> *Recommendation 21: Greater priority should be given to the capital requirements for residential child care to accelerate replacement programmes.*
>
> *Recommendation 22: Local authorities should set standards for the maintenance, repair and general furbishment of residential child care establishments (including standards for the time taken to effect repairs). Local authority inspection units should monitor the achievement of these standards in local authority and independent establishments.*
>
> *Recommendation 23: Accommodation for young people with disabilities should be designed to ensure space for equipment and wheelchairs to be used in comfort.*

Food

3.3.11　Young people and children in residential care appear to be well fed. Many homes have cooks although in the small ones the care staff and the young people prepare and serve the meals between them. Where this is possible it works very well; for instance, in one particular voluntary sector project the staff are all qualified social workers and see the meal preparation as an integral part of the overall task. Cooking and cleaning are important parts of the care task, and whoever meets these needs should be valued members of staff, or residents. When they are specialists, they often bring a very useful experience of life and good sense. The kitchen should not be a remote food production line, but a vital central place where people can congregate, and which can become a centre for informal discussion and counselling. The way food is presented reflects the value of the recipient and details such as putting hot food on warm plates are very important.

3.3.12　The kitchen should not be locked. If there is a large store it may have to be locked. Locking all food away, as some homes do, conveys a real sense of deprivation and does not at all feel like home.

3.3.13　Some homes make valiant efforts to encourage preparation for independence; by, for example, asking those young people in bed-sits within the home to prepare their own food. These meet with varying degrees of success, and there are some administrative difficulties in financing the arrangements. It is disappointing that by and large young people still have little direct contact with shops and supermarkets and the buying of food. Too much food is still delivered through formal purchasing arrangements, which deny young people and children the opportunity for ordinary learning at first hand.

> **Recommendation 24: Young people and children should always have access to simple food such as fruit, tea, juice, biscuits, bread, milk and cereal.**

> **Recommendation 25: Formal purchasing arrangements involving the bulk buying of food and other domestic materials should be avoided.**

Personal Care and Clothing

3.3.14　For most young people and children with special needs, high quality care and training in life skills are essential components of appropriate provision. To set a good standard of physical and personal care is a basic pre-requisite of residential child care; yet it is not easy to give it proper attention in the turmoil of some homes. Some staff lack the necessary life experience; training is important in this area as in others. Personal care is easily neglected in residential homes because shifts bring staff change, and there is sometimes a reticence to openly discuss mundane but personal matters. For personal development and self-worth it is, however, important and staff should always attend to these aspects of care allowing children to make choices and create their own personal style and identity.

3.3.15　Clothing arrangements have moved on from the days of the legendary order book, although many officers-in-charge are concerned that the amount of money available is insufficient. The right balance has to be struck in giving children the opportunity to take a pride in their appearance, and being realistic as to how much money they will have in the future, and how much their families can afford. Some staff share out the clothing budget as a regular monthly sum, while others agree to purchasing as and when necessary. A routine allocation should be made on a scale everyone can understand, but there are difficulties in homes with a high turnover and a need for a lot of initial kitting out and clothes for school. There could be yet more involvement of young people in the acquisition of clothing; accompanying younger children to a range of shops to choose and pay for clothes is an important experience for a child and justified use of staff time. Some homes insist that all the children wear school uniform. This does not seem to be an education department policy nor a school policy but a social work department requirement. It would be a matter for concern if this led to the young people being marked out in some way.

3.3.16   Young people and children should have things that are actually their own. If they do not have even simple possessions then they have nothing to value, and may feel themselves valueless. They have to establish their own identity and gain respect for themselves as individuals. One example, encountered during the review, was of a teenage girl whose apparent possessions were a wide range of toiletries, shampoos and bubble bath. Upon investigation these proved to be empty; she couldn't buy full ones, and the bulk buying arrangements led to a single supply of shampoo of a kind she did not like. To be an owner of a lot of empty bottles summed up the way that adults were helping her to think of herself. The remote bureaucracy that insisted on a single type of product was ignoring the importance of individual choice.

3.3.17   The whole question of choice permeates good residential care. Choosing the activity in the evening, choosing the food to be eaten, choosing your own clothes and possessions are essential ingredients for a satisfying life. It is part of the staff's task to increase the range of choice, and those staff who work in the home need the support of their colleagues at headquarters, or in the supplies department.

Recreation and Transport

3.3.18   Residential units differ greatly in the budget available to them for activities for the young people in their care. Residential schools tend to have access to a wide range of outdoor and craft activities, and the means of transport to enjoy these. In smaller children's homes these facilities are less likely to be available, and sometimes staff are hard pressed to find the money to finance activities beyond hiring a video. A balance has to be struck between providing enough activity for young people and allowing them time and space to organise their own lives. It is clearly important that staff should have the resources to enable them to encourage young people, who may have missed out on social and leisure experiences. A wide range of appropriate social and leisure experiences is also crucial in promoting the development of children and young people with special needs, encouraging special interests in sports and hobbies.

3.3.19   Staff must also be able to provide some structure to the activities of the weekends and holidays. If resources do not allow them to do this then the growth of boredom, frustration and anger amongst the young people and children should come as no surprise.

3.3.20   Many young people in residential homes have real ability and the potential to achieve in sport, music and other creative activities; many are being financially supported and encouraged to participate. When young people are able to identify their own interests and needs in this respect, staff do encourage them. Sadly, however, many young people have no significant interests, and greater emphasis needs to be placed on the importance of encouraging young people to have interests outside the residential unit, and to develop their social and recreational skills. The encouragement of these activities should be a specific part of the care plan for individual young people and children. Staff training should include the development of skills in this area.

3.3.21   It is a matter of constant complaint that children's home transport has a local authority, voluntary agency or sponsor's logo on the side panels. Young people and children feel very strongly about this because they feel they can go nowhere without being labelled as 'children from the home'. It is quite different from the identification of ordinary school buses or other public transport used by the population as a whole. However meritorious the authority or agency it must recognise that it is impossible to put a logo on the outside of the bus or car without putting a label on the young people and children on the inside. It could be argued that some charitable donations of transport depend on agreements that the sponsor's name should be displayed. Other arrangements for publicising the sponsor could and should be made. Young people and children are right to object; their status as residents of a children's home or school should be treated as a personal and private matter.

> *Recommendation 26: Recreational budgets should always be sufficient to provide structured weekend and holiday activities.*
>
> *Recommendation 27: Transport for residential child care establishments should not be marked in such a way as to distinguish it from an ordinary car or bus.*

IV. EDUCATION

Young people and children should be actively encouraged in all aspects of their education, vocational training or employment and offered career guidance. Their individual educational needs should be identified and met.

Educational Needs

3.4.1   All children have a right to statutory schooling appropriate to their needs and should be offered opportunities for continuing further and higher education beyond statutory leaving age. Educational progress at whatever level is a powerful means of promoting a sense of self worth and equipping the individual for a richer and more satisfactory adult life. Failure and disaffection with previous poor educational experiences should not be accepted as an excuse for allowing the individual to opt out of schooling.

3.4.2   When a young person or child comes into care there is a tendency within social work and other agencies to perceive her or his needs as being solely social work needs and a failure to identify, and to plan in sufficient detail how to meet, the range of educational, health and developmental needs common to children in care and all other children. Where children or young people have to change schools when admitted to care, it is essential that effective, and speedy arrangements are in place for exchange of information and records. All too often, little or nothing is known about a child's educational attainments and valuable time is wasted on reassessment, to the frustration of the child or young person.

3.4.3   Social work departments are responsible for identifying care needs of individuals, including those related to their education. Education authorities have a duty to identify children's educational needs and to make provision for them. Close collaboration is required between the responsible members of social work and education departments if the range of services required by individuals are to be provided in the most effective and efficient way. Where children have recorded special educational needs or are subject to formal assessments of future needs, there are statutory procedures which involve parents, educational psychologists, medical officers and other relevant professionals. Clearly where such children and young people are in care their key worker and social worker have important contributions to make to those procedures.

3.4.4   Where children and young people are happily settled in their school, care arrangements should be made to enable them to continue in a setting which provides stability and continuity. Most authorities have set up some arrangements of this kind. To ensure continuing effectiveness staff in school have to be briefed and arrangements set up for collaboration. There are many good examples of harmonious and productive relationships between staff in respite care facilities and in schools. For example, complicated, but well planned arrangements among staff in a respite care facility, a school and a hospital has allowed one family to continue to provide for two members with complex special needs.

3.4.5   It is particularly important that care and education staff work together to make effective arrangements for, and prepare children and young people for, admission to new schools, units or classes or to further educational facilities. Plans should be made from the earliest possible moment and actions taken to prevent last minute ad hoc, and generally unsatisfactory experiences for the individual.

3.4.6   There is considerable educational research evidence to show that troubled and troublesome young people gain self reliance from a sense of achievement which is greater the higher the level of attainment they reach in basic educational skills. A large proportion of young people coming into residential care already have school difficulties often accompanied by a history of truancy and behavioural problems in class. Many local authorities put a good deal of planning and energy into evolving youth strategies involving both education and social work departments, with the object of keeping young people out of care. Once the children are admitted to care, however, this collaboration seems to become less effective. There must be a conscious effort to ensure that this inter-departmental collaboration is maintained throughout the period the child remains in care.

3.4.7   In some homes school work is taken seriously and there are plenty of examples of young people being encouraged to work for examinations. Too often, however, where it is considered that young people are unlikely to achieve well, that view is self-fulfilling and school work tends then not to be given high enough priority. Staff need the time and understanding to help young people to achieve their potential and frequently feel they do not have the opportunity for this because of pressure of time and space. It is important that staff are seen to value education and that young people are encouraged to take educational achievement seriously. Befrienders can play a useful role in this regard.

3.4.8   The care and management of young people excluded from school presents real problems to homes which do not themselves provide education. Young people living in such children's homes who have been excluded from school are usually cared for during the day by the staff of the unit. This is a regular feature of life in some residential units and places particular pressures on care staff. It demands, for example, a greater staffing level and expertise from staff during the day than would otherwise be needed.

3.4.9   The provision for young people who were excluded from school is described in 28 of the statements of functions and objectives evaluated for the review. Some indicate that staff would supervise the completion of work provided by the school, while others expect young people to help with chores around the house. Some made temporary arrangements for young people to attend a nearby social work resource which provided education. Most who addressed this issue recognised that these arrangements were unsatisfactory and that there should be a wider range of resources for children who were not able to attend mainstream schooling.

3.4.10   In the survey conducted for the review a total of 49 homes (51% of homes not providing education) had had children excluded during the summer term of 1991. The median percentage of numbers of exclusions varied regionally. The lowest was 11.5% and the highest 27.5%.

3.4.11   Exclusion from school cannot help the resolution of the emotional and behavioural problems facing many young people in care and it is strongly questionable whether it is as appropriate a response as its frequent use might seem to indicate. It is felt that responses to behavioural problems could be a good deal more positive and constructive. The development of a joint approach between schools and homes to develop more effective strategies for maintaining them in school would be more helpful to the child or young person and would benefit the staff in the residential home. For example, greater use of learning support staff allied to supportive action by care staff is likely to be more effective and to influence the future behaviour of the child or young person.

3.4.12   It is common for statements of functions and objectives to indicate that care staff enjoyed good relationships with local schools but only 56 (43%) of those evaluated for the review gave any details about arrangements for liaison. In only 25 statements (19%) was there reference to progress at school being considered at reviews. Links with schools normally relied on the key worker making regular contact in respect of individual children; an appropriate practice that seems to vary in quality. More effective arrangements can be made. For instance, each home in one area has the services of a link teacher who monitors the child's progress in school and helps with homework or extra tuition as necessary. This teacher also attends child care reviews and is able to provide any relevant information on the child's progress in school. This practice also means the young persons feel someone else cares about their educational progress and achievement.

3.4.13   In 20 statements, arrangements for children to undertake homework were described, usually indicating when it should be done and that members of staff would be available to give encouragement and help if necessary. This was mostly mentioned by units who provided long-term care for children and who aimed to provide a family atmosphere. Some of these units mentioned that key workers would attend parents' nights for key children or would take part in fund raising or social events at the schools. This is good practice, and it would be helpful if in-service training for care staff were to give insights into the educational provision offered in the schools attended by their children and if it could be explained how they might support a child's progress at school within the context of the home. Residential staff could contribute to the in-service training of teachers.

3.4.14   Where children and young people have learning difficulties or face some barriers to learning, due to physical disabilities or sensory impairment, educational and care staff should collaborate closely to ensure that they are setting compatible aims and that each is approaching the individual's learning in a consistent manner. Key workers should join teachers and other members of the multi-disciplinary team to assess the special educational needs of individuals, and to plan, implement and evaluate their educational programmes. Methods such as home-school diaries and regular telephone contact ensure that key worker and teacher are kept in regular contact and exchange relevant information; the objective is that they should work together for the good of the child. When children require specialist support and intervention by therapists and educational psychologists, key workers and teachers should receive guidance support and advice from these professionals to allow them to contribute to the specialised programmes. Thus if a child who cannot talk is using a sign system such as Makaton, everyone in daily contact with that individual should be trained in its use. It is unlikely that children and young people with complex special educational needs will make satisfactory progress unless everyone involved in their education and care adopts the same or similar practices. In particular, collaborative approaches are essential for children with multiple impairments or disturbing behaviours.

3.4.15   When children and young persons, aged 2-18, require exceptional educational provision, as a result of special educational needs which require continuing review, then the Education Authority should open a Record of Needs for them. Special education needs arise from learning difficulties or barriers to learning, or a mixture of both. The Record is a legal document containing a short assessment profile, a statement of special educational needs, ways in which the education authority proposes to provide for them, including which school is to be attended. The Record is a confidential document accessible only to the directorate of the education department, the child's parents or guardians and staff responsible for the child's education. The Record of Needs is subject to regular review and is amended when there are changes in circumstances. For example, changes of school must always be entered on the Record. In good practice care staff should contribute to the assessment and review procedures where they have a contribution to make to the child's education. The information contained in the Record of Needs, updated by records of reviews, should form the basis of an individualised educational programme to which parents, care staff and relevant support staff should contribute in addition to teachers. It is important that education authorities and social work departments should consider ways of integrating recording procedures with more general review arrangements.

3.4.16   For children with Record of Needs and within 9-18 months of statutory school leaving age, assessments of future needs are a statutory requirement. At future needs assessment meetings the final years of a young person's schooling are discussed and consideration is given to how a child might best be prepared to take advantage of the placement opportunities available. Clearly the young person should be engaged as fully as possible in the process with the advice and support of family and case workers. Further information is available in the Parent's Charter document "Guidelines for Parents of Children with Special Educational Needs". Social workers, parents, key workers and the young people themselves share these assessments of their future needs. This is an important time to help these young people to prepare for adulthood and particularly to continue with educational opportunities where their education has been interrupted by periods of hospital treatments and/or illness, or they have slower learning patterns due to disabilities.

3.4.17   Young people in residential care should always be encouraged to take a positive view of their future employment and careers. Staff should be adequately trained to advise and support them. They should understand how the careers advisory services work, and should have made appropriate links with all the agencies concerned with vocational training. Similarly, some staff should make appropriate links with employers and job centres. The way in which this is managed should not be left to ad hoc initiatives of individual staff, who may or may not be well-equipped to undertake this work effectively. Each authority and agency should have a considered and constructive plan geared to maximising the employment and career futures of young people in their care. Currently there is little evidence of well-thought schemes in this regard. Local authorities in particular, though other agencies as well, should actively consider schemes in which young people in the care of the authority can be employed, at least for a time, by the authority. This employment could be in any department, including the social work and education departments.

> *Recommendation 28: Local Authority Education and Social Work Departments should review their arrangements for overseeing the educational needs of children in care, including those excluded from school. They should consider the designation of senior staff in both departments with responsibility to oversee the education of children in care.*

> *Recommendation 29: Education and social work departments should ensure that arrangements are made for rapid exchange of documents and advice on the educational programmes and progress of individual young people and children in order to prevent time being wasted in unnecessary educational reassessments.*

Dual Registration and Planning

3.4.18   Of the 154 establishments covered by the survey 26 provided education, which accounted for 4 out of every 10 children in residential care. All 26 units were registered with a social work department in addition to any registration which they might require as a school.

3.4.19   Those residential homes providing education tend to be larger than those that do not, the median size of homes with education was 36 compared to 12 for those offering care only. They also fulfil a variety of roles and cope with a range of need; the basis of the placement may be statutory or non-statutory. There are other residential independent schools where children in care are placed and which are not registered with the local social work department. In order to ensure common standards and more effective co-ordination it is sensible that, where the social work department intends to make regular use of a particular residential school, that establishment should be requested to register with the local authority under the Social Work (Scotland) Act 1968 as well as registering as an independent school under the Education Acts. If all authorities adopt this suggestion it would mean that any school in Scotland which wished to attract social work placements would need to seek registration with the local social work department.

3.4.20   One important practical implication is that all such residential schools would, in future, have to prepare a statement of functions and objectives which would be subject to scrutiny by local authority social work and education departments as well as the Social Work Service Inspectorate and HMI Schools.

3.4.21   It seems rather anomalous that local social work departments have responsibility for registering and inspecting all residential establishments providing personal care for adults, but do not have a responsibility for inspecting the personal social care provided for children in all residential schools. The Child Care Law Review recommended that there should be (recommendations 7 and 8);

> "A new duty on the proprietors and persons in charge of independent residential schools to safeguard and promote the welfare of children resident in the establishment; and

> "New responsibilities on the local authority in the area where the school is situated for ensuring that the welfare duty is properly discharged."

The independent schools organisations should be consulted on the extent to which the principles and recommendations in this report would assist themselves and local authorities in the exercise of these duties if they were imposed. The proposed new duty should extend to hostels for young people and children attending school away from home.

> **Recommendation 30: Where the local authority have a responsibility or interest in the placement of a child in a residential educational establishment, that establishment should always be registered under Section 61(1) Social Work (Scotland) Act 1968.**

V. HEALTH

Young people's and children's health needs should be carefully identified and met; they should be encouraged to avoid health risks and to develop a healthy life-style.

Assessing And Meeting Individual Health Care Needs

3.5.1   Because of their circumstances young people admitted to care have frequently not received adequate continuous or consistent health care advice or developmental attention and for many it will be necessary to improve this situation. Many will have changed addresses frequently and changed GPs, others will have missed the benefits of the school health service for one reason or another. On admittance to residential care, the health needs and requirements of young people should be addressed and monitored and appropriate remedial action taken where necessary. Young people and children who have had several placements since reception into care are at increasing risk of having their needs overlooked because no single person has had oversight of their health care.

3.5.2   There is a considerable amount of change underway in the systems of delivering both health care and social care. This presents the danger that a lack of understanding amongst the agencies may lead to the needs of this particularly mobile and vulnerable group of children and young people not being addressed as effectively as they might be. Some homes have established excellent working arrangements with their local general practitioners and others in the health service. Some of these arrangements may be affected by the changes. Some authorities and agencies may wish to consider how to gain most benefit from the new arrangements such as the New Patient Registration Examination offer that will be available to new full residents.

3.5.3   The freedom-from-infection medical upon reception into care is not comprehensive and while it may be necessary, it is no substitute for a full medical examination and assessment. There is great value in a full developmental health assessment for all young people during their first weeks in care and this should involve a parent where possible. Such an examination will provide a clear basis for any necessary remedial attention.

3.5.4   The Child Care Law Review recommended that

> "Care authorities should be authorised by statute to arrange developmental health assessments of children on admission to care - where the child's stay in care is likely to extend beyond 6 weeks - and at regular intervals thereafter."

This, however, should be part of the health care provision already started for the young person. The emphasis therefore should be placed on swift transfer of records where that is appropriate and recognition that the general practitioner, community services and school health service may all have access to relevant information and have a role to play. Young people may remain with their original general practitioner or temporarily register with a local general practitioner. In the latter case they would, after three months, have to decide whether to register fully. It is important to achieve maximum continuity of medical care and thus reduce the number of examining doctors and maximise the formation of good relations between patient and doctor.

3.5.5   The health needs of children with disabilities who are receiving short-term or respite care need to be considered, but full medical examinations and assessments are not required for periods of less than 6 weeks. Children having respite on a long-term planned basis should do so in a similar way to any child going to stay with friends or family.

3.5.6   Young people should have the right to consult a general practitioner without going through staff or explaining the reasons for the consultation. In addition it is important that young people should, wherever possible, have some choice as to the doctor undertaking examinations.

3.5.7   Individual health needs should always be considered at child care reviews which should also ensure that there is no ambiguity about who is to take responsibility for ensuring that the young person's health needs are met.

3.5.8   On a more general level the responsibility for ensuring that the systems are working effectively lies both with the local authority and the health board. Because of the vulnerability of this mobile group and because of the changes that are taking place there is a need to ensure that there is good liaison at a senior level in both health boards and local authorities to oversee the effectiveness with which the health needs of young people and children in care are being identified and met.

> *Recommendation 31: Local Authorities and Health Boards should review whether they have adequate liaison arrangements in place for overseeing the effectiveness with which the health needs of children in care are identified and met.*

General Health Education

3.5.9   Education in health care issues is an ongoing process for young people within residential units and generally this includes discussion of accidents, hygiene, sexuality and contraception, and the dangers associated with alcohol, solvent and drug abuse. Some local authorities provide clear guidance and training on these matters whilst in others care staff feel they have to find their own way. Several residential units working with young people who are about to leave care have developed excellent programmes and personal health care is significant in such programmes.

Smoking

3.5.10   Homes take a number of approaches to smoking. Some have established very clear policies and practices which minimise smoking amongst young people and staff. In some only young people over 14 are allowed to smoke and then only if they have their parents' consent. In other homes any child with enough pocket money to buy cigarettes (which would generally include 8 year olds) seems to be free to smoke so long as he or she does not do so in a bedroom. This is deemed to be a safer policy than forbidding smoking and "driving it underground with the risk of starting fires". In many homes staff smoke openly and on occasion share their cigarettes with the young people in their care. Field social workers also sometimes give cigarettes to children.

3.5.11   For many young people and children in care smoking is an established habit amongst friends and family. They do not come into care in order to be weaned off smoking nor to be lectured and constantly "corrected". However young people and children in care have a right to protection from other people's smoke and protection from being led to misunderstand the dangers of smoking.

3.5.12   The dangers are clear. One in six Scots die because of their smoking. The prevalence of smoking amongst young people aged 10-15 in Scotland has always exceeded that of England and Wales. Exposure to other people's smoke increases the risk for lung cancer by 10-30%. Children exposed to passive smoking have a higher than expected incidence of middle ear disease, and an increased risk of wheeze and respiratory symptoms. There is also evidence that there is an increased risk of meningococcal disease in children who live with smokers. The dangers of teenagers who smoke 3-4 cigarettes becoming trapped into a career of smoking lasting their sadly foreshortened lives are well known.

3.5.13   Residential child care staff ought therefore to be able to have complete confidence in showing their disapproval of smoking, and ought to show that disapproval. The young people and children in their care should not be given ambiguous messages and should be clearly discouraged from smoking. Cigarettes should never be used as a reward. Children in care should not be given cigarettes as a gift by any member of residential or field staff. Staff - whether they are residential, field or managerial staff - should not smoke in children's homes.

3.5.14   Fieldworkers should take care to fully support the residential staff's stance, and should themselves never smoke in front of young people and never offer young people cigarettes.

3.5.15   Some have suggested that sharing cigarettes is a good way of defusing situations and forming relationships. There are better ways - as the many staff who do not smoke have shown.

Recommendation 32: Local authorities and voluntary organisations should each have a clear policy on smoking and children in care. These policies should prohibit staff from smoking in residential homes (including fieldworkers and other staff visiting residential homes); should prohibit staff from smoking in front of young people offering young people cigarettes; and should clearly discourage smoking amongst young people specifying limited rules and conditions under which young people are allowed to smoke. The policies should aim to establish a position in which homes and residential schools are smoke-free environments for both staff and young people.

Recommendation 33: "Who Cares" should revise its statement to clearly discourage smoking and draw attention to young people's right not to be exposed to passive smoking.

Sexuality

3.5.16   Most people experience some kind of difficulty with the development of their sexuality. Moreover adolescence is a time for experimentation, and, inevitably since most young people in residential care are adolescents, issues of sexuality feature significantly amongst the complex matters with which residential staff have to deal.

3.5.17   Staff in homes are generally well aware of the main issues, but they are too often untrained and uncertain how to proceed. In some cases they lack clear guidance from managers. Staff need training that enables them to be comfortable with their own approach to issues about sexuality, so that they can help young people in a relaxed and confident way. Such training should include the special needs of young people with disabilities. Courses are available through a variety of organisations.

3.5.18   For many young people in residential care there can be the additional factors of low self-esteem, past experience of abusive relationships and therefore often a lack of clarity about sexual boundaries, and sometimes a lack of confidence in avoiding inappropriate sexual behaviour. Sometimes self-worth is so low that there is a complete lack of concern for the future results of present risky behaviour.

3.5.19   Staff should clearly discourage young people and children under the age of 16 years from having sex. It is also important to face the reality of the extent to which sexual activity occurs, and to approach the programmes within the home, and individual counselling and discussions, in ways which allow the young people to speak honestly about their experiences.

3.5.20   Discussion and education should take place within a general programme that includes life styles, sexual health, alcohol, drugs and assertiveness. It may well not be appropriate for staff in a residential unit to deliver formal programmes as such; it may sometime be appropriate to involve somebody from outside but most of all staff in daily contact with the young people should be properly equipped to engage in such discussion in order to maximise opportunities as they arise.

3.5.21   Issues about HIV/AIDS may raise particular anxieties for young people and for staff. Social Work Services Group has issued draft guidance on children infected or affected by HIV and this includes guidance relating to residential care.

3.5.22   Managers must provide staff with clear support in handling the many difficulties associated with these issues. If they have reasons for concern they should seek medical advice and support; this may include the possibility of making condoms available to some young people. It is important that residential staff should not feel that they have to deal with these complex and anxiety provoking issues on their own. Local authorities and voluntary organisations should ensure that their staff have adequate guidance and training.

Recommendation 34: All residential child care staff should have some training on sexuality and some key staff in adolescent units should be trained to take a lead role in ensuring that staff in the unit are confident in dealing with the complexities of the issues involved. The training should include training in relation to HIV/AIDS.

Drug, Alcohol and Solvent Abuse

3.5.23   As part of the health education programme, young people should be made aware of the dangers to health caused by drug, solvent and alcohol abuse. This type of abuse is common among young people generally, and it is unrealistic to expect that young people in care will be immune from these forms of behaviour. They do present particular problems of management to staff who have to deal with the unpredictable and disruptive behaviour of young people who are intoxicated or under the influence of drugs or solvents.

3.5.24   Care staff are uniquely placed and indeed have a clear responsibility to promote positive and healthy life styles for the young people in their care. An effective preventative strategy is dependent upon care staff themselves being well informed about these issues and having the requisite counselling skills to be able to offer consistent and realistic guidance and support. Whilst serious abuse may require help being sought from specialist staff outwith the unit, the care worker's role will nonetheless be central to any treatment plan. Local health education staff should be able to assist with the preparation of materials for training and guidance and should be consulted.

3.5.25   In respect of alcohol it is important that young people should see models of sensibly limited drinking rather than perceive there to be a choice between abstention and drunkenness. It is therefore appropriate for adults to consume small amounts of alcohol in the home on special occasions and to discuss with the young people their own approach to alcohol - assuming, of course, that it is a sensible one. Young people are often more influenced by other young people than by adults and "Who Cares" or local young people could assist in promoting sensible habits and in making guidance and training materials more effective.

> *Recommendation 35: In-service training programmes should include elements that will assist care staff to feel competent and confident in working with young people experimenting with alcohol, drugs or solvents. Local authorities which have not done so should prepare practice guidance for care staff in relation to handling drug, alcohol and solvent abuse and appropriate information leaflets for young people in care.*

VI PARTNERSHIPS WITH PARENTS

Young people and children in residential homes and schools should be cared for in ways which maximise opportunities for parents continued involvement, and for care to be provided in the context of a partnership with parents, wherever this is in the interests of the child.

Links With Parents And Family

3.6.1 Research indicates very clearly that where strong family links are maintained there is a greater likelihood of the child in care returning home. The point of admission and the first six weeks in care are particularly critical in establishing the expectations of those involved and in laying the groundwork for future rehabilitation. The care plan must be established and agreed promptly, with particular attention to helping parents and the young person or child feel they have a role to play.

3.6.2 Social work managers and field and residential staff are well aware of these requirements and generally direct their efforts to achieving them. Many residential staff consider that their potential role in this regard is underestimated. Residential staff are in a strong position to form effective relationships with families and to promote a well-timed return home.

3.6.3 Many parents find it easier to visit a residential unit than a foster home and most units do facilitate visits and ensure that young people have somewhere private to take their family. Ideally there should be overnight accommodation suitable for parents and relatives or for visiting ex-residents. In some homes redundant staff flats are used for this purpose. Some units have the capacity to provide a meal or a cup of tea and where this happens it is greatly valued by parents. Even where units are welcoming however, parents are likely to feel uncomfortable and careful thought needs to be given to ways in which they can be made to feel that their presence is positively valued. Most young people will eventually return home, but even when they do not the relationship with their family is likely to be a significant one and every effort must be made to help sustain it as positive and meaningful.

3.6.4 Parents should be told immediately of any significant happening in their child's life by the unit staff - of illness, accident or absconding. This does not always happen. Some parents have learned that their child had absconded several days after the event when the police have come to the door and this is clearly unacceptable. They should be encouraged to attend hospital and school appointments with their child where possible in order to retain an understanding of their child's general welfare. Parents should be given a copy of the functions and objectives statement when their child enters care, and should be given an explanation of the house rules.

3.6.5 Parents often have a sense of failure and embarrassment about having a child in care; they feel very much alone and enormously distressed. Parents are as likely to need help and support over this period as their children and it is important their needs are not neglected; there may well be a need for emotional support. They should certainly be given common courtesies. They may often think they are treated as irrelevant and feel very lonely. Where parents' support groups exist these are highly valued as a means of allowing parents to talk to other people in the same situation.

> *Recommendation 36: Parents should be given a copy of the functions and objectives statement of the home before or when their child is admitted. They should be given an explanation of the general organisation and any house rules. They should be able to arrange a confidential discussion with their child (unless there is clear evidence that this will be detrimental for the child) and similarly with a member of staff. They should be kept informed of developments in their child's life.*

Parents' Rights And Responsibilities

3.6.6 Parents of young people and children in care also have rights and responsibilities. Recommendation 17 states that they should have the right to make a complaint in confidence and paragraph 3.2.22 suggests that they could have a right in local procedures to require that a review be held when a review has not been held within the time limits; this is reflected in recommendation 19.

3.6.7   Some agencies and homes are very sensitive to the rights of parents but few have set out clear statements as they have for young people in care. There would be considerable advantage in doing so in order to clarify for parents what their rights and responsibilities are and also as a means of assisting their engagement with the continuing care of their child and the staff involved. Where it is available parents clearly appreciate the support of other parents and local and national support groups would be valuable in ensuring that the system is as open as possible to their experience and views.

> **Recommendation 37: Local authorities and agencies providing residential child care should draw up statements of rights and responsibilities for parents of young people in care. These should be issued to parents on or before the admission of their child.**

> **Recommendation 38: The formation of local and national organisations for parents of young people and children in care should be encouraged.**

VII. CHILD CENTRED COLLABORATION

Young people and children should be able to rely on a high quality of inter-disciplinary teamwork amongst the adults providing for their care, education and health needs.

3.7.1   If young people and children in residential care are to reach their full potential then agencies and individuals who are charged with caring for them need to work well together. This is no easy task. Not only are there many bodies which make decisions about young people in residential care, for example children's panels, social work departments, health boards, voluntary and private organisations, but there are many more individuals whose actions and work affect the care experience of these young people, for example care workers, managers, teachers, cooks, builders, inspectors, doctors and others. The quality of care, and the quality of decision making is determined, not only by their individual actions, but also by the extent and manner of their collaboration.

3.7.2   Adults have a clear, sometimes sharp, sense of their distinctive roles and responsibilities. These distinctions are often not perceived by young people and children; they place immense trust in adults, and assume that they work closely together. In some instances their trust is well placed, and there are examples of good collaborative working in the daily routines of most authorities and agencies. However, in general, the quality of inter-disciplinary teamwork is, at best, patchy. This may be symptomatic of insufficient priority being given by managers of different agencies to promote a strong framework of inter-disciplinary working.

3.7.3   It was clear from submissions to the review, and from visits, that many professionals consider that children and young people suffer because the various agencies have not collaborated in making and maintaining arrangements appropriate to all their needs. Poor collaboration may arise from a lack of training; training provides the information and knowledge of networks required, and can also provide the necessary confidence in the value of one's role, plus an appreciation of the value and nature of the roles of others. Effective inter-disciplinary team work depends on all members openly and honestly exchanging information and working together on this information, plans and evaluation. Unless the professionals agree to work towards shared objectives, there is little chance of the child or young person and his family understanding the nature of the arrangements made and the options open to them.

3.7.4   Young people and children in care should receive at least the same standard of education and social, emotional and health care which parents in general would want for their children. This objective is unlikely to be achieved without positive collaboration between departments and professional disciplines. Providing an effective framework for this collaboration is the responsibility of senior managers. Social work services must be a fundamentally integrating factor in society, not a segregating one; senior managers should be pre-occupied with how they, and their organisation, are working in collaboration with other agencies. The responsibility for collaboration, however, is a shared one and all agencies require to be committed to collaborative working if it is to be successful.

> *Recommendation 39: Local authorities should consider local joint training initiatives for education, social work, and other disciplines on collaboration in providing good quality residential child care.*

VIII. A FEELING OF SAFETY

Young people and children should feel safe and secure in any residential home or school.

The Importance of Feeling Safe

3.8.1   This principle is a fundamental one. If young people and children do not feel safe and secure then the task of meeting their emotional, developmental and other needs can hardly be begun.

3.8.2   Admission to care - perhaps particularly residential care - is inevitably a lonely and frightening experience. To cope with it young people and children need support and care and they need confidence that they are not at risk of attack or victimisation by other children, staff or visitors. Indeed their needs are so great that they will sometimes even accept abuse if they can also get some comfort. Pre-requisites of good residential child care therefore include provision that homes are staffed and managed in such a way that residents are safe and feel safe. Staff should be carefully selected and supervised so that the likelihood of abuse is minimised (see Chapters 4 and 5). Where appropriate staff should be trained in the physical management of children and young people with physical disabilities to allow them to carry out care routines and programmes in ways which inspire feelings of safety.

3.8.3   The establishment of an environment in which young people feel safe and secure is the first priority. This entails the establishment of routines within the unit and definitions of acceptable behaviour which are understood by everyone - both staff and young people. Security is provided for children and young people through continuity of care and experience in an environment which is predictable and consistent. Physical and emotional security are the basis for healthy growth and development and residential care must provide this before anything further can be achieved.

Emotional and Behavioural Difficulties

3.8.4   In most homes it is clear that young people and staff do feel safe and comfortable with each other and well engaged with tasks of emotional and developmental growth. In others they seem rather frightened of each other and only tentatively able to approach each other on emotional and developmental issues. In many homes the situation lies somewhere in between and doubtless varies over time.

3.8.5   No evidence was found in the review of regimes such as that which operated in Staffordshire and was known as "Pindown", nor was there any evidence of young people or children being abused by staff. The visits paid to homes were inevitably relatively brief, however, were not inspections and many homes were not visited. As a whole it is clear that within residential child care abuse may occur and go undetected. There is no one answer to this problem. Better staffing, new inspection arrangements, more openness to involving outside adults, such as parents, volunteers and other professionals, in the business of the home - all of these matters will help. It is essential that the momentum towards greater openness is maintained. One particular aspect to stress is that staff and others should not hesitate to inform the police of any concerns that they have. The police, with their expertise, and responsibility for investigation are best placed to judge the seriousness of any allegation and to take appropriate steps. They may also have other information.

> **Recommendation 40: Persons receiving allegations, or suspicious themselves, about possible abuse of young people or children in residential care should inform the police without hesitation.**

3.8.6   It is concerning that an atmosphere of tension and alienation is sometimes found in homes. Submissions to the review referred frequently to the stress of dealing with emergency and inappropriate admissions, aggressive incidents, and complex situations; to staff having neither the time, resources or training to handle these demands in ways that could provide young people with the necessary sense of security and reassure everyone involved that matters were well organised and under good control.

3.8.7 One measure of a sense of feeling safe is the absence of violence. The survey showed that a total of 39% (46 homes) experienced physical violence against staff members during a one month period. The proportion of units having had a violent incident was highest among secure units with 80% (4 out of 5) units experiencing staff assault. There had been an incident involving violence to staff in 11 or 58% of residential homes with education. Three of the 4 reception centres had had a violent incident as had the large unit (with 143 places) for children with special needs. Among units not providing education a third reported at least one incident of violence towards staff.

3.8.8 The occurrence of violence was only partly related to the size of the home. An incident was reported in 35% of homes (without education) caring for under 10 children, in 31% of homes with 10-30 children and in neither of the 2 homes with over 30 residents.

3.8.9 Of the 30 homes experiencing violence, 8 reported 5 incidents or more, the maximum being 23. Five of the 8 were children's homes caring for 10-20 children. Two of the 3 reception centres experiencing violence had had 5 incidents as had 4 of the 11 homes with education. Only one home and 5 children's units reported more than 5 incidents. A few children's units were therefore experiencing more violence than most homes with education. The pattern of violence to staff seems only partly related to size and to the type of unit.

3.8.10 The reason for violent and aggressive behaviour may not always be immediately apparent and it will rarely be accounted for by one factor. Possible contributory factors that have been identified include the young person's reaction to admission into care, peer group pressure, testing out staff, inconsistent response by staff and under-manning of units at critical periods of the day.

3.8.11 Whatever may be seen as contributory factors, staff need to have the time, skill, confidence and support to deal appropriately with potential and actual violent behaviour. The overall organisation of the functions and objectives of units is very important in this regard. Larger authorities should be able to organise their homes such as to be able to provide the appropriate level and kind of support to young people with different needs; there is no ideal blueprint for this organisation, authorities are rightly developing a range of approaches. Smaller authorities may need to consider in more detail how best they should collaborate with other authorities and with independent agencies in planning provision. However well planned the homes, training will be vital. Training in conflict avoidance and managing violent behaviour, underpinned by clear policy and practice guidance are basic pre-requisites. Some local authorities and other agencies have good guidance material for staff and induction training in what to do and what not to do, others do not.

3.8.12 However able and well-trained staff are, they will not be able to prevent escalation to violence if staff numbers are insufficient to handle the events which arise in some homes. Staffing levels should therefore be determined in the light of the functions and objectives of the home and not solely on the basis of the numbers of residents.

3.8.13 Alcohol and solvent abuse are contributors to violence in homes. Agency policies must be clearly laid out for each home so that staff can act with confidence to prevent incidents escalating.

3.8.14 Aggressive behaviour can be due to frustration and feeling misunderstood. Children with communication problems can feel overlooked and isolated when no effort is made to allow them to function and relate to others as all children should. Training for staff in communication skills and the special needs of some children can help to avoid such behaviour.

3.8.15 There are no clear figures of police call-outs to homes, but in some units a police presence is a regular feature several times each month. At some points in a very few units the situation has developed to a point where staff have lost their self confidence and the situation has felt out of control. This is clearly a frightening situation which is very difficult to repair or reverse. The position may be worsened by deteriorating relations with neighbours or exacerbation of problems by the actions of other young people in the locality. In some serious situations the only answer may be closure. This emphasises the point that prevention is all important.

3.8.16   The solutions to these problems lie mainly in staffing, training, management and planning and we make relevant recommendations in Chapters 4 and 5.

Setting Limits to Behaviour

3.8.17   All young people and children (and adults) need to have limits set for what is acceptable behaviour and what is not. Without these they do not feel safe. This is an important part of growing up and of living in a free society. For some homes and for some individual young people and children it can present particular difficulties.

3.8.18   The survey conducted for the review examined the range of possible actions which could be taken to deal with any difficulties arising from young people's behaviour. A number of measures was identified and each home was asked which it used. The results are shown below:

Table [3.1]

Measures Used to Control Children
and Young People

Frequency of usage in Descending Order	No Homes Taking	% Homes Taking
Restricted Leisure Activities	99	82
Early to Bed	89	74
Physical Restraint	81	67
Control of Pocket Money	75	62
Extra Tasks	56	46
Isolation	24	20
Withholding of Normal Clothing	13	11
Grounding/Staying in Unit Boundaries	7	6
Reduction in Family Contact	6	5
Loss of Home Visits	5	4
Reparation for Damage	5	4

Physical restraint in relation to young people who lose control was reported as being used in three-quarters of all homes. The use of physical restraint is stressful for everyone involved. In units where it becomes a regular feature of life, staff become exhausted and demoralised. There are personal, and physical risks involved in restraining angry and distressed young people and there is great emotional strain in "talking down" some very tense situations. Some staff become accustomed to using restraint. Staff are also keenly aware of the risk of being accused of assault by the young person. These stresses and anxieties highlight the vital importance of good support and supervision.

3.8.19   Isolation is used in a higher proportion of residential homes with education, being used in 26% of them and in 17% of units not providing education. It is used in 2 of the 4 assessment/reception centres that responded to the postal survey.

3.8.20   Among units providing no education the proportion using isolation as a sanction is higher in larger units. Of units caring for less than 10 children, only 11% use isolation while among those taking 10-20 and 20-30 children 16% and 31% respectively use this sanction. One large unit providing education for children with special needs uses this sanction. The use of physical restraint and isolation would appear therefore to some extent to relate to the size and type of population, though the nature of the relationship is not clear.

3.8.21   Some homes use "time out" in another home as a form of control. Removal to another home should only be necessary in extreme situations and should not be a regular occurrence. In particular it should not be a routine method of managing trouble. If the practice were to continue, then it would undermine improvements being made possible through better staffing, training and management.

3.8.22 Some establishments, especially small children's homes, use no sanctions except staff disapproval. Effective controls depend upon the effectiveness of disapproval, not on physical restraint. For disapproval to be effective approval must in the first place be important. Young people and children must know they are cared for if they are to care about themselves and their behaviour. They can only learn respect for others, through respect for themselves. They must also learn the boundaries of acceptable behaviour. The key skill so often is to be able to show disapproval of the behaviour without disapproval of the person.

3.8.23 Children and young people with intellectual disabilities are sometimes admitted to care because they have disturbing behaviours which are not susceptible to change by ordinary measures. Research has suggested that a multi-disciplinary approach is most effective, especially when it involves adaptation to the environment of the child or young person to encourage appropriate ways of behaving. Gentle teaching has been found recently to produce beneficial improvements in the way in which children respond. Making provision for such children and young people requires support for care and educational staff through in-service training and from specialist staff.

3.8.24 Some local authorities have produced explicit codes of conduct on acceptable and unacceptable sanctions and paramount in these statements is the protection of young people and the prohibition of sanctions which degrade or humiliate. There is wide variation in the extent to which disciplinary arrangements are made explicit. The approach to these matters is closely linked to the home's philosophical approach but is not always clearly spelled out.

3.8.25 Issues of therapy are too often compared with sanctions and control. There has been concern about the possible prevalence of false "therapies" following the Leicestershire incidents and it is necessary to state clearly that sanctions and control are quite different from therapy. It is impossible to consider providing any form of therapy for a young person or child who is not in the first place being adequately cared for and protected from abuse.

3.8.26 As with many areas of residential child care there are wide variations in practice and the difficulties of spreading knowledge about good practice is inhibiting the proper development of the services. There is need for a positive effort to bring practice up to the standard of the best and a first stage to achieving this will be a common code of do's and do not's. Agency guidelines in this area include the elements which could best be included in a simple central guide, which could appropriately be issued by the Social Work Services Inspectorate as a guide to practice. A draft guide is provided in Appendix A for consultation. A working group with members from local authorities and independent agencies, and from homes with education and homes without, should review the responses and refine the guidance. Psychologists working in the field of social skill development and related areas can bring important understanding to the issues involved and appropriate solutions. The working group should include a psychologist.

3.8.27 Guidance and procedures without training will be ineffective. Training for all staff in the development of skills in setting clear limits for acceptable behaviour, and the use of appropriate sanctions and controls is essential. Induction training, essential for all staff, should include training in the establishment's approach within the context of agency policy and guidelines; it should emphasise the importance of consistency in the staff team's approach, and should include information on how staff can raise concerns about any inappropriate sanctions or controls they observe or suspect are being used by other staff. In addition to having clear guidance and training it is essential to ensure that the guidance is followed. This is the responsibility of all staff and managers. Managers should review all incidents to see what lessons may be learnt and should discuss limit-setting in regular supervision sessions. Staff should have access to a procedure whereby they may raise concerns about inappropriate sanctions or controls they consider may be being used by others. The Inspection units should, once the guidance is issued, set up procedures to inspect whether it is consistently adhered to.

Recommendation 41: The Social Work Services Inspectorate should convene a working group to draw up guidance on sanctions and control in residential child care. Once the guidance is issued local authority inspection units should review at least annually the adherence by each home to the guidance and should involve young people and children in this review. They should also review staff training undertaken in respect of implementing the guidance.

Recommendation 42: Statements of functions and objectives should differentiate clearly between 1) care provided, 2) sanctions and control permitted, and 3) any therapy available in the home. They should include details of any specialist training in therapeutic work.

Absconding

3.8.28 Young people and children may run away from a home for different reasons. They are less likely to run from a home when they feel safe and secure.

3.8.29 There has been recent attention to the issue of the numbers of young people who abscond from residential care and a report was produced in July 1991 by Social Work Services Group[8] following an inter-agency working group which included representation from the police. Absconding is by no means a general feature of life in residential care and most young people who abscond do so from a small number of units. Young people who do abscond are likely to do so more than once and in the main are very emotionally damaged young people. The report stresses that social work departments, in recognising their full management responsibility to such persistent absconders, will need to discover the causes of absconding not only by looking at the behaviour and emotional state of the individual child but also at whether there are deficiencies of any sort in the establishments in which children are placed. It says "in some circumstances the child's absconding is an attempt at self preservation and in these circumstances therefore has not to be condemned." The working group recommended a new approach for dealing with absconders and this has been operating since September 1991.

3.8.29 Some young people who abscond do feel they are punished on their return, for example by deprivation of privileges or by being "frozen out" by staff. Residential homes and schools need to think carefully about their practice in dealing with returning absconders and to recognise that a warm welcome back is important.

3.8.30 As a rule the majority of young people who abscond do not travel far. There is no evidence of a significant number of children in care running away to London for instance. There is evidence in Scotland and other parts of the UK that young people and children tend to abscond from certain homes and not others. The reasons may be complex but should be investigated by managers and where appropriate the registering authority for each residential home or school where the pattern arises.

Recommendation 43: Local authority managers and Inspection Units should routinely gather information on absconding rates from residential homes and schools and investigate patterns, causes and solutions based on the recommendations of the Absconding Working Party.

Secure Accommodation

3.8.31 Secure accommodation is a necessary and important part of our child care provision. Like all residential child care provision it needs to be used appropriately and in a way which best meets the needs of the individual young person. The arrangements for the provision of secure accommodation and the admission criteria are detailed quite specifically in legislation and regulations[9]. These were introduced in 1983, defining secure accommodation as 'accommodation

---

[8] "Absconders From Child Care Establishments; Proposals For Improved Liaison Arrangements." The Scottish Office, 1991.

[9] Children and Young Persons, Residential And Other Establishments Scotland, The Secure Accommodation (Scotland) Regulations 1983.

provided in a residential establishment for the purpose of restricting the liberty of children. The regulations require that every establishment wishing to provide secure accommodation be approved by the Secretary of State. In addition there is an SWSG code of practice[10] which guides the care of children and young people in these establishments.

3.8.32 Currently there are 7 units in Scotland providing a total of 84 places. These units tend to cater for children requiring secure accommodation care on a medium to long term basis. Most young people in secure accommodation are there by virtue of a supervision requirement of a children's hearing. A sizeable proportion of young people are also confined in these establishments by the provisions of Sections 205 and 206 of the Criminal Justice (Scotland) Act 1975. Sentences under Section 205 are for those persons including children who have committed murder. Sentences under Section 206 are for other serious crimes which would have attracted a prison sentence in the case of adults. A number of young people are also held on remand or transferred on the authority of a Director of Social Work.

3.8.33 The question of the provision and use of secure accommodation in Scotland was last reviewed in 1987. At that time there was general agreement that the provision was adequate for current and future needs.

3.8.34 However since then there has been a much greater use of secure accommodation for short term purposes, for instance, from the courts, police apprehensions, or intensive care for some youngsters for a limited period prior to transfer into open accommodation. Throughput is now double the rate it was 10 years ago. There are increased numbers of girls for whom places are required, and changing perceptions of the type of education which should be available within the context of secure accommodation.

3.8.35 Since 1984 considerable progress has been made in reducing the use of unruly certificates by encouraging local authorities to recommend to courts the use of secure accommodation as an alternative to penal establishments for the remand and assessment of children. Improved dialogue and co-operation between local authorities, the police, procurators fiscal and the courts have resulted in a substantial reduction in numbers of children detained in Scottish penal establishments under "unruly certificates". The figure was 137 in 1985, followed by an annual decline to only 8 in 1989. In 1990 and 1991 the figure rose to 30 and the provisional figure for the first half of 1992 is 12. This compares favourably with the position in England and Wales where the number of unruly certificates is in the order of 1500.

3.8.36 Placement in prison, however, cannot be said to be in the best interests of any young person. There are sometimes difficult decisions to be made about individual children and serious questions to address about the handling of exceptional cases. Secure accommodation is not always effective for an extremely violent young person who for example persistently and seriously assaults staff or fellow detainees. The aim, however, should be that no young person under the age of 17 is placed in prison.

> **Recommendation 44: The Scottish Office should review the future needs for secure accommodation following a national inspection in 1992/93 including an assessment of placements and use, distribution and condition of present provision and the quality of care provided. This review should also inform consideration of what further may be done to reduce the number of unruly certificates and also to avoid the imprisonment of young people of 16 or younger.**

[10] Code of Practice: The Use of Secure Accommodation for Children: The Scottish Office April 1985.

CHAPTER 4

Staffing and Training

General

4.1 If ever there was a labour intensive industry it must be residential child care. Staff are the really important ingredient in the care package offered to children and families; much depends on their personal and professional skills and knowledge, and the confidence which comes from them. Buildings can be improved, bedrooms can be made more attractive, but staff make or break the system. Staff are the key resource, but currently are trained too seldom and too little, insufficiently supported and sometimes appointed too casually.

Determining Salaries And Conditions

4.2 Specific proposals for changes in pay or conditions of service are beyond the remit of this review. The Convention of Scottish Local Authorities has established an inquiry to examine these issues which is expected to report this year. Nevertheless there are two important points to make.

4.3 Firstly, current salaries and conditions of service are generally insufficient to attract and retain staff able to undertake the complex tasks often involved in residential child care, and with the qualifications and training that should be brought to bear. Staff in residential settings should be able to earn as much as they would in field settings for the deployment of the same qualifications and skills. Improving salaries without improving conditions of service is unlikely to significantly improve retention of qualified staff. However, the nature of residential child care is such that it will be difficult to reduce the working week any further. Children need care from adults whom they know well, and with whom they have plenty of contact. One national voluntary organisation has kept the working week at 45 hours since that was first introduced in 1973. In other agencies the hours have been reduced to the extent that, if the working week were to come down much further, then children would have contact with so many adults, over so short a period, that they would have difficulty developing satisfactory relationships with the staff. Because of this other models of staffing residential child care should be explored, including models where longer hours can be offset by other benefits.

4.4 A handbook[11] prepared by the Wagner Development Group and published by the National Institute For Social Work in 1990 offers practical guidance in addressing this requirement for flexibility. This approach identifies a set of questions designed so that the answers will enable managers to determine the range and volume of skills required to meet the aims and objectives established for each residential home. They identify the peaks in demand for staff time and the troughs or quiet times. They enable managers to consider the costs and benefits of different approaches to staffing and shift systems. The handbook shows how staffing might be calculated for different types of homes and discusses the creation of rotas. The model can be of considerable assistance to officers-in-charge, and to senior managers, in the process of balancing the needs of young people and children in residential care, the interests and concerns of residential staff, and the costs of providing a service.

4.5 Secondly, remuneration must reflect the different demands made in different settings. Residential care does not make uniformly even demands for qualifications, skill or experience. It is not that the demands are different for different client groups. Some homes for elderly people, or for people with mental illness, or learning disabilities, require just as high a level of qualification and skill as some children's homes. There is probably no realistic way of determining a national system of categorisation that can truly reflect the complex variations. Within any one category, the

---

[11] Wagner Development Group (1990 Staffing in Residential Care Homes, NISW).

functions and objectives of individual homes will be very different and need to be considered in determining salaries and conditions. The skills required vary so much, and the demands placed on staff can be so different, that staffing structures, salaries and conditions should be determined differentially. This requires considerable local flexibility. The tasks in residential care can sometimes be more complex and demanding than those in field settings, and it must be possible for this to be reflected in remuneration if a good quality of care is to be established and maintained.

> **Recommendation 45: In general, salaries and conditions of service of residential child care staff should be improved in order to attract and retain staff with sufficient ability and qualifications. Employers should recognise the range of skills required in different homes, and ensure that there is flexibility to determine salaries and conditions of service differentially.**

Staff Selection

4.6 Systems of staff selection which are properly organised, and properly conducted, are essential to building any good staff team. The vulnerability of many of the young people in residential child care, and the dependency they must have on the staff to whose care they are entrusted, are such that very particular care in staff selection should always be taken. In some organisations providing residential child care the staff selection processes are detailed and thorough, but this is by no means true of all appointments. Most authorities and agencies have, as has been noted, considerable difficulty with staff recruitment. Some agencies experience considerable difficulty in recruiting staff, and all agencies have difficulty in retaining staff, particularly if they have obtained a social work qualification. There is little use made in Scotland of staff supplied by private agencies, but quite extensive use of the appointment of temporary staff; either because the employer is uncertain about the appointment, or in order to temporarily replace staff on secondment or leave.

4.7 The Department of Health has established an inquiry into the selection and recruitment of staff in children's homes, chaired by Mr Norman Warner. Though its recommendations will technically relate only to England, the subject of the inquiry is of relevance in Scotland and its findings should be considered here.

> **Recommendation 46: The Scottish Office should consider the applicability in Scotland of the recommendations of the Warner Inquiry into the selection and recruitment of staff in children's homes, and issue appropriate guidance in due course.**

The Lack Of Training

4.8 The importance of training for residential child care staff and managers has been emphasised throughout this report. In 1990 the position with regard to qualifications of staff in local authority residential establishments for child care was as shown below.

Table 4.1 Staff Qualifications in 1990

	Total	Social[1] Work Qualified		Other[2] Qualifications		None of these	
		No	%	No	%	No	%
Officers in Charge	110	45	41	34	31	31	28
Asst. Off. in Charge	211	63	30	39	18	109	52
Houseparents	1372	88	6	70	5	1214	88
Teachers	76	15	20	61	80	0	–
Other Staff	214	17	8	19	9	178	83

1. CQSW and CSS
2. Other social service, nursing, nursery nurse, occupational therapy, youth and community qualifications, teaching and instructors qualifications.

Source: SWSG Statistics

4.9   The key points in these figures are: –

- over a quarter of officers in charge and one half of assistants have no qualification at all;

- in these grades there are about one-third who have social work qualifications;

- of those with qualifications in these grades about 60% have social work qualifications;

- of other care staff 88% have no qualification at all.

4.10   The survey commissioned for this review covered voluntary and private establishments, as well as the local authority. The findings showed that for all sectors in 1991 83% of care staff had no relevant qualification and only 14% (a total of 259 out of 1,902 care staff counted in the survey) had a social work qualification (Diploma in Social Work or equivalent).

4.11   At present, in most authorities and agencies, residential child care is being provided by a workforce which is largely unqualified. It is clearly a priority to build up and better equip staff to run Scotland's homes and residential schools for children and young people in the future. There are many problems in the way - not least the size of the reservoir from which so much has to come. Improvement in the quality of care requires smaller homes with more staff, better trained managers, more of whom have experience of residential child care practice, more training officers, quality assurance teams and inspectors, SVQ assessors, consultants and administrative staff. These demands fall on an existing pool of staff which is ill-equipped to do the task, and which is constantly being drained by the departure of many of those who obtain qualifications. The objectives should not simply be to retain and develop the staff who are in post, but must also be to attract back some who have moved into other areas of social work, or who have taken a career break. The problems of a lack of training and difficulties in improving the level of training are by no means new issues.

4.12   The literature review describes the history of the low levels of training and qualification amongst residential staff. Despite the creation of a number of training courses in the late 1950s, residential child care staff remained largely untrained through the 1960s. When generic social work training courses and departments were established joint training for residential and field workers was strongly favoured. Courses leading to the new Certificate of Qualification in Social Work (CQSW) were often criticised, however, for not offering enough to students wishing to work in residential settings with young people and for not giving enough consideration to the specialist needs of residential workers. Moreover there were major problems in meeting the training needs of the very large numbers of residential staff involved. In the 1970s a new qualification, the Certificate in Social Service (CSS), was established which introduced a more work-based training which was better able to meet the needs of residential staff. It was also generally a better preparation for management than the Certificate in Social Work. However, this new certificate was seen as providing a lower qualification and it did not provide for the numbers originally envisaged.

4.13   The 1990s have seen the introduction of the new Diploma in Social Work, replacing both the CQSW and the CSS, and the development of the Scottish Vocational Qualifications (SVQs). The Scottish Vocational Qualifications provide a means of validating the skills of staff developed through experience or training. They play a very important role, but if the level of training of residential child care staff is to be improved that cannot be achieved simply through a system of validation; it must come from increased training, which may be appropriately allied to a system of validation.

4.14   In several other European countries the particular skills required for residential care are better recognised than in the UK. Well based training courses have been established, leading to nationally recognised and accredited qualifications. In some countries field and residential social workers train together for an initial period of up to two years, and are thereafter trained separately in their specialty. In the United Kingdom the possibilities of adopting this approach were effectively abandoned twenty years ago. It is debatable which will prove, in the longer run, the better approach; however, the creation now of a separate approach to training would not fit well with new training developments in the UK. Moreover it would run counter to the importance of integrating residential child care within the whole range of child care services.

4.15   It is clear from the history, and present difficulties, that securing a higher level of qualification and training of residential child care staff will not be at all easy. Over recent years local authorities and other agencies have approached the issue in a number of ways; some have met with at least partial success, and there are a few homes with virtually a fully qualified workforce. These are the exception.

4.16   Effective change will only be achieved through sustained progress in several key areas. The first two key areas are the need to increase the number of staff with a Diploma in Social Work or equivalent, and the proportion of staff assessed as competent at SVQ level 3. National targets for the proportion of residential child care staff qualified in these ways should be set and these are proposed in the next section. The third key area is that of induction training. The importance of induction and in-house training has been stressed in studies and reports for two decades. Much more substantial progress than has been made is required if there is to be any effective improvement overall. Recommendations in regard to induction training follow the next section. The fourth key area is the need for some small secondment schemes which will allow staff to work for a period of some years in residential care and which will allow some residential staff to work in other settings for similar periods. The fifth key area is the importance of improving support for residential staff, particularly through supervision. The sixth is the need to enhance the status of residential child care staff. Recommendations in relation to all of these are made below.

4.17   Unless progress is made on each of them then the overall position will not change. If induction and in-service training is not improved, or if support for staff is not improved, or if the status of residential child care staff is not enhanced, or if there are not more opportunities for staff to move between field and residential settings, then strategies for increasing the level of qualifications through secondments and other initiatives will fail because staff who are or become qualified will continue to leave. The tasks facing residential staff will not become less complex and, if anything, the requirement for training is likely to increase. The recommendations in this chapter are aimed at providing a platform for the sustained progress that is required. It would, however, be quite wrong to await an influx of trained staff; priority must be given to advances in training which are more immediately realisable, and the key to this is induction and in-service training.

National Training Targets

4.18   National targets for training in residential child care are called for in order to provide a focus for positive training strategies at all levels. Social Work training programmes provide the appropriate core discipline, though the coverage of specific skills required in residential care needs to be improved; there should also be wider recognition of the applicability of skills and knowledge attained through other qualifications. All staff should have appropriate training for the work in which they are engaged. Residential child care can benefit from a range of skills. Psychologists, Home Economists, Teachers, Occupational Therapists, Community Education staff, and others have training and experience which can be relevantly deployed in residential care. Several local authorities and voluntary organisations have recruited staff with these qualifications and skills and they should continue to do so. National targets should be adopted for the proportions of staff required with different levels of training. The targets recommended will take several years to reach on a national basis, but, given the complex and important tasks in residential child care, they are wholly appropriate.

4.19   Some authorities and agencies are progressing towards having 100% residential child care staff with relevant qualifications. This is an appropriate goal. It is also quite appropriate for homes and schools to vary in the proportions of staff they have with different qualifications; this is consistent with the widely varying roles they play. If residential child care is to meet the essential requirement to provide skilled care, rather than simply 'warehousing', however, then the variation must be limited. Two targets should be set: firstly, for the proportion of staff with a Diploma in Social Work or equivalent, and, secondly, for the proportion assessed as competent at level 3 on the Scottish Vocational Qualifications in social care.

4.20   All senior care staff, including officers-in-charge, should have a relevant qualification. However setting a target for, say, all officers-in-charge to have a Diploma in Social Work or equivalent might lead to difficulties in the most effective targeting of secondment opportunities; moreover other qualifications are relevant and it should remain possible for staff with qualifications in, for instance, psychology or teaching to become officers-in-charge. The immediate target at a national level should be for a proportion of senior care staff to hold a Diploma in Social Work, or its equivalent.

4.21   Residential children's establishments are faced with meeting needs which are amongst the most complex and challenging of any social work service. Some argue that only a small proportion of staff need to complete the Diploma in Social Work, but that does not seem consistent with the increasing evidence about the complexity of the task. It is generally accepted that field social workers should all be fully qualified, and it is far from clear that they have more demanding or complex responsibilities. When young people and children are admitted to residential care it should be because they need the special care and skills available; the staff should, therefore, be equipped to deliver skilled care.

4.22   Some authorities and agencies may be able to achieve a high level of qualified staff through a reduction in the numbers of staff involved and concentration on the provision of skilled care for a small number of young people. Nationally this may prove more difficult to achieve in practice. The introduction of the specific grant for social work training in local authorities has included a proposed target of 30% of residential care staff holding a Diploma in Social Work or equivalent. This is appropriate, but the longer term aim should be that 60% of residential care staff are qualified at this level; that may not be achievable before the next decade. An additional target should be set that the majority of senior care staff, 90%, should be fully professionally qualified social workers.

4.23   It is important that social work qualifying courses should give more attention to the skills required for residential care of children. An expert group has examined the residential child care content of qualifying training courses following the Utting Report and the CCETSW are preparing guidance about the teaching of residential child care. It would be appropriate for this to be part of better developed learning opportunities and training for social workers in group care settings of all kinds. These should, however, highlight both the similarities and differences of work in different settings. Training should also emphasise the importance of integrating residential child care within the wider range of social work child care services rather than within other residential services. Some social workers receive little training about residential care or groupcare with any client group during their qualifying course and have no practice experience of it. It is an essential part of social work service and it is important, therefore, that all students on courses leading to a social work qualification should have an assessed group care placement.

4.24 The development of the Scottish Vocational Qualification (SVQ) provides a means for ensuring that the competence of other staff can be assessed and recognised; where the assessment indicates the need for further training, this can be planned for. Building the scheme such that staff may develop along a continuum is important. CCETSW is developing this, in collaboration with others, and this is very valuable. The qualification is entirely worthwhile in its own right. Some may wish to move on to further training, some may not. The significance of SVQ is clearly considerable in residential child care. It could do much to enhance the quality of services and the career structure of the workforce.

4.25 It is essential, however, that the assessment of the various levels is underpinned by high quality training and supervision. There is a danger, with increased emphasis on measurable competencies, that less measurable skills and insights, essential to good social work service practice, are neglected. The major emphasis and development of resources should be in training and development of new skills, as well as in the validation of existing skills. To ensure that homes can provide skilled care it is appropriate that the majority of those staff who do not have a full social work qualification should have been assessed as competent at SVQ3 which is also consistent with the award of HNC. In introducing the specific grant for training of local authority social work staff a target was proposed of 60% residential child care staff to have achieved level 3. In the medium term that is an appropriate target though it may be overtaken since, in the longer term, the proportion should reduce to 30% as the proportion of those with Diplomas in Social Work rises.

Recommendation 47: Local authorities and independent organisations should aim to achieve a position in which 30% of all residential child care staff, and 90% of all senior residential child care staff hold a Diploma in Social Work or equivalent.

Recommendation 48: Local authorities and independent organisations should aim to achieve a position in which 60% of residential child care staff are assessed as competent at HNC/SVQ level 3.

Recommendation 49: All students undertaking Diploma in Social Work courses should have at least one assessed group care placement.

Induction Training And Probationary Appointments

4.26 Residential child care staff are in a very powerful position in respect of vulnerable young people and children, because of this, and because the tasks involved are complex and challenging great care should be taken over their appointment and preparation. Selection procedures should certainly be improved but they can never be fool-proof. It is by no means a straight-forward matter to determine whether or not someone is really suited to work in residential child care. It is vital that care staff should genuinely like young people and children and be in all other ways suited for the task. To establish this with certainty requires more than even the best selection procedures can offer. It is therefore appropriate for there to be a period of probation before new staff are confirmed in their appointment. For this to be effective and positive it must be tied in with sound induction and probationary training and assessment. These should enable staff to complete the first steps towards the attainment of higher levels of training.

4.27 Staff who have not previously worked in residential child care should serve a probationary period of one year. Before they are confirmed in post new staff should be assessed as performing at level 2 of the Scottish Vocational Qualifications (SVQ) for Staff in Residential and Day Care Services, or above. If they are unable to meet this test of competence they are unlikely to be able to become good residential child care staff.

4.28　The position of induction training for residential child care staff in Scotland is very varied. Some agencies provide a consistent and carefully designed programme for all new staff which follows on from careful selection; many do not. Some staff seem to have little or no induction training. Induction training is important for any enterprise as the training officers of high street stores seem to know well enough. The complexities of the residential child care task, the vulnerability of the young people and children, the importance of consistency in how staff handle matters, and the need for staff to work in collaboration with others all require that induction training should be of a high quality and consistently delivered. Of all the training requirements the greatest priority should be given to induction training.

4.29　Induction training should be formalised and standardised for each agency and new entrants put on a set of steps that can lead to further training. There are presently 2,000 residential child care staff in Scotland's child care establishments (excluding cooks, handymen and ancillary posts). More than 300 are officers in charge and assistant officers in charge. If there is annual turnover at the rate of 25% for the remainder, then induction training is required for 400 people a year. Induction training needs to be more than just an introduction to the staff and daily routines. It needs to cover a general understanding of residential child care, and, in more depth, the functions and objectives of the particular home, handling admissions, relationships with young people and children, their parents, other professionals, responding to crises, handling issues of sanctions and control and a range of other matters. This requires induction training equivalent to two working weeks for each member of staff; this is a substantial but realistic challenge. Most of the training should be completed before the new member of staff is included in the shift rota, though some of the training may take place in the home. It might be possible to offer the induction training before employment begins as a condition of employment; for people already in full-time employment it could be undertaken as an evening and weekend activity. It is more likely, however, to constitute the first two weeks of a new employee's time.

4.30　Large authorities may be able to phase recruitment, particularly if other changes bring more stability to the work force. A key figure in arranging the induction is the line manager, and it is critically important that all line managers have available to them a prepared induction programme. They must also play a key role in further training and support for staff during their probationary year and subsequently. Residential staff are inevitably rather dependent for their development on the resources available within the home or school in which they work; office based staff are much more able to undertake occasional day courses and conferences without having to arrange specific changes to the shift rota etc. The role of officers-in-charge is thus particularly important and should be developed in collaboration with the agency's staff development resources.

> **Recommendation 50: All residential child care staff should have 2 weeks' induction training. This should be the training target given first priority.**

> **Recommendation 51: New staff with no previous experience of residential child care, should be appointed on a probationary basis. Their appointment should be confirmed after one year only when assessed as competent at SVQ2.**

Achieving The Training Targets

4.31　The government, local authorities and others have already taken initiatives towards the achievement of these training targets. The new specific grant for training for local authority residential staff provides the main vehicle enabling local authorities to meet the additional requirements and will also provide a means of monitoring progress. Voluntary organisations have also taken initiatives, but they do not directly benefit from the introduction of the new specific grant and they require more immediate assistance in order to meet the costs of seconding staff.

> **Recommendation 52: Funding for voluntary organisations to second staff to qualifying training should be increased.**

4.32 There is currently a shortfall in the number of practice placements available for social work students in Scotland. This could become a significant obstacle to meeting training targets in general. More practice placement units dedicated to residential child care should be created. The responsibility for meeting the costs of practice teaching lies with local authorities except in regard to the voluntary sector; practice teaching placements in the voluntary sector are funded by Scottish Office grant through CCETSW. The costs of providing new practice placements in residential child care has already been made eligible expenditure for specific grant funding for local authorities, as they would be new developments rather than replacements. It is important that the voluntary sector contribution should be developed further. The creation of good practice placements will assist in encouraging newly qualified staff to enter residential child care. It will continue to be cost effective and important for the quality of the service for authorities to recruit staff who are already qualified and changes in the overall attractiveness of residential child care work should ensure that it becomes a positive career choice.

> **Recommendation 53: Training consortia should consider the development of additional practice placements in residential child care, working to ensure that there are sufficient placements to meet the needs of their area. Funding should be made available for additional practice placements in the voluntary sector, specialising in residential child care.**

4.33 Additional teaching resources are required if effective progress is to be made towards the national targets. This will require to be funded in a variety of ways, but it is appropriate for the Scottish Office to initiate developments and it is recommended that funding be made available for additional lecturing resources to be appropriately distributed across Scotland.

> **Recommendation 54: The Scottish Office should fund additional social work lecturing resources to be distributed across Scotland to promote the required expansion of social work training.**

4.34 A major difficulty in residential child care is ensuring that knowledge of good practice is disseminated and used; staff working on rotas are unable easily to take time off to attend seminars or meetings, and there are insufficient opportunities for the exchange of information on good practice or for individual or team development. The national targets for volume training are necessary, but will take some years to achieve and are not sufficient in themselves to ensure that a good standard of care can be provided. It is more important in the immediate term that staff benefit from good quality induction and in-service training, and opportunities for development and sharing knowledge of good practice. These will lay the foundations for effective progress towards the national targets.

4.35 To assist in the development of good quality induction and in-service programmes, and in the dissemination of knowledge and its application in practice, it is recommended that a centre for consultancy and development in residential child care be established. This centre should be funded by the Scottish Office, initially for three years. Its remit would be broadly to design and deliver consultancy and staff development opportunities to residential staff in voluntary agencies and local authorities and to develop learning materials. Employers, colleges and voluntary organisations should be consulted first on the specification for the centre's remit.

> **Recommendation 55: The Scottish Office should fund the establishment of a centre for consultancy and development in residential child care. The specification for the centre should be drawn up after consultation with relevant bodies.**

4.36 The complex tasks of residential child care also require the development of more specialised and advanced training courses and academic institutions should consider the development of advanced training courses to equip staff for managerial and consultancy work as well as direct practice.

Supporting Residential Care Staff

4.37 Local authorities and voluntary agencies have generally sought to increase support for residential care staff in recent years. Several have made changes to the organisation of their management responsibilities, specifically with a view to improving the line management support available to residential homes. These developments are very welcome. However residential child care is demanding work, often stretching staff to their professional limits and involving considerable professional and personal stress. Despite some improvements many residential staff continue to feel insufficiently supported for the tasks they undertake. Generally, and particularly with regard to supervision, residential staff still seem to receive less support than field staff.

4.38 Many staff express a feeling of low morale and concern that they are inadequately rewarded and supported for the complex tasks they face. In support of this, there is some evidence that sickness levels in residential child care are higher than in other social work and social care settings. One Scottish local authority analysed the number of days lost through sickness amongst the salaried staff in its social work department; the average for all staff was 4.48%, but in children's homes the rate was the highest of any staff group at 7.81%.

4.39 Residential staff should always receive regular supervision from their line manager, covering both their day to day work and professional development. Such supervision is not a luxury; it is an absolute prerequisite for good practice and sound management. Regular individual supervision is often difficult to achieve with the constraints of a staff rota, and is extremely vulnerable to any kind of crisis, large or small. But it is the main means by which staff can integrate learning and experience.

4.40 Some homes receive strong support from outside consultants, but overall the impression is that this has rather reduced as a source of support over recent years. Some agency staff seem almost to disapprove of it on the grounds that it may distort management communication. That is a very blinkered view. Good communication is of course essential, but it must be communication in which staff feel involved and supported. Units where staff morale appears highest are those where there is frequent and regular discussion, where staff feel they can be frank with colleagues about their concerns. In the best homes staff meetings, case discussion meetings, sessions with an individual consultant, shift hand-over meetings and individual and group supervision are well used and important. When there are crises within these homes staff feel that they can trust one another and be confident of consistent responses. When this trust is absent the results are demoralising and can be damaging for staff and young people.

4.41 Within each home there needs to be close attention to how communication occurs and a disciplined approach to ensuring that there are no false economies. Young people in distress need to feel the security of confident adults and this has to be achieved within the staff team by careful team building. This can often be helped through the deployment of an outside consultant.

> *Recommendation 56: All residential child care staff should have regular supervision and agency managers should initiate systems to monitor the provision of supervision.*

Secondment

4.42 Many staff may want to work in residential child care for a period but not for their whole career. Indeed there is a strong case for ensuring that staff do not work all their lives in residential care, in order to ensure that they do not become "burnt-out" or institutionalised. There are also some staff in residential child care who were appointed at a time when they were expected, and expecting, to undertake rather different work with a younger group of children. Agencies may therefore need to consider secondment schemes for staff. There is considerable value in the development of approaches which enable some staff to move into another area of practice after a period of ten or fifteen years.

Enhancing The Status of Care Staff

4.43   Strengthening the role and standing of the keyworker can help young people and children feel that they themselves have more power and influence over decisions. Parents too, have more confidence if they deal with one person with whom they can establish a relationship. Some qualified and experienced staff in particular, have been able to develop this role into one of considerable significance for the young people concerned. In some homes the role of keyworkers has been developed to the point that they are the key professional working with the young people and sometimes with their families as well. There are also examples of keyworkers playing an active part in helping to place children from residential care to foster care, being involved in assessment, matching and ongoing support.

4.44   These developments are welcome and to be encouraged. In most homes there is considerable scope for further development of the role of key workers. Key workers may play a part before, during and after a young person or child is admitted to residential care and could develop their role in relation to families. Such developments should be underpinned by appropriate training and recognition of the staffing implications. In some instances the needs of individual young people can best be met by transferring full case responsibility from the field social worker to a qualified keyworker in the residential home. These are exceptions and a note of caution is required. The vulnerability of young people to exploitation is considerable and care must be taken that no single adult is able to form an exclusive relationship with a young person which prevents her or him from having significant relationships with other adults. Nonetheless there are circumstances in which it is appropriate for keyworkers to carry full case responsibility and formal acknowledgement of this will help to enhance the role of residential care staff.

> **Recommendation 57: Qualified key workers should be able to hold full case responsibility within agency review systems, when this is in the best interests of the young person or child. When this is done, care should be taken to ensure that young people and children continue to have regular contact with other professional adults.**

4.45   The part played by residential staff cannot be developed if all the decisions are effectively made by field staff. In some homes residential staff do have authority to make a wide range of decisions regarding the young people's needs and development; in others their scope is very limited. In some agencies the budgets for meeting developmental needs of young people are controlled through the fieldwork offices in order to plan and monitor expenditure across all types of care. This has the effect of requiring residential staff to seek field staff's authorisation to meet costs of what are essentially basic care requirements. Some argue that this is necessary because the field staff know the young person's background and can keep an overview of these expenditures as she or he moves to other placements. This information should, however, always in any event be passed by the field staff to the residential staff and is no reason for withholding financial authority from the care staff. If residential staff are not even given the authority to assess basic care needs and to determine how best to meet them, then their status will never be enhanced and young people will feel that they are being cared for by powerless second-class professionals. To prevent this the general level of authority held by residential staff must be increased. They are in a much better position to assess the young person's needs, and very probably better able to manage a budget effectively and efficiently.

> **Recommendation 58: Residential care staff should carry authority and budgetary responsibility for individual expenditure to meet the basic care, recreational and developmental needs of the young people and children in their care.**

4.46   One further way of enhancing the standing of residential staff would be to improve their capability and capacity to prepare written material of a high standard. Most residential staff are skilled in verbal and non-verbal communication with young people; many indeed are highly skilled and generally this is an area in which they outshine field staff. Verbal communication, however, needs to be supported by written records through adequate case notes, daily logs and reports of critical incidents. Many of the most important decisions regarding young people are made at meetings such as child care reviews and case conferences and these rely extensively on written reports. Residential staff's influence on these therefore depends to a considerable degree on their ability to produce good quality written reports. Often they do not find this easy. They usually lack clerical support and very often lack even access to a simple word-processor or typewriter. Many also lack confidence in writing reports and it is a matter in which very few get much practice or have any training. Field staff by comparison have much easier access to typists, spend a lot of time writing reports and develop a relative fluency. Written reports and records are integral components of the overall professional task of caring for young people and are also important means by which residential staff can communicate their knowledge, insights and assessments. Each home should have a word-processor on site and basic training for appropriate staff. Local authorities should consider the scope for increasing the level of clerical support available to homes.

Recommendation 59: The Scottish Office should finance and commission training material in report writing for residential child care staff and teaching on the subject should be included in training programmes.

CHAPTER 5

Management, Planning and Inspection

The Management Responsibility

5.1 It is a management responsibility to turn around the current rather negative position of residential child care; a management challenge to be worked at over years, not weeks. Improving salaries and conditions of service, training and staff support are all necessary but, not by themselves, sufficient steps to improving the quality of residential child care. Positive and committed management is a key requirement in delivering the extensive improvements required. In most authorities management support appears to have improved in recent years, but it still requires strengthening, particularly in relation to planning, leadership and quality. Without leadership, programmes of change and improvement are likely to be ineffective. It is surprising that so few senior managers in social work services are women; a better balance would be likely to promote a better standard of care. Women are an underused resource in the management of residential care and in other areas of social work service management. Women may not be encouraged by line managers to seek managerial posts and may not put themselves forward. In view of this the Scottish Office is funding a survey of the training needs of women managers so that these may be effectively targeted by training provision. The report will be available in 1993.

5.2 Some call for a new vision for residential child care, some for an expansion, some for a reduction. These views are simplistic. What is required is not a new vision or sudden change, but a clear commitment to the provision of consistently good quality residential child care. A commitment to bringing all homes up to the standard of the best and to the continuous improvement of the service. Such a commitment to continuous improvement must be at the heart of the management and planning of residential child care, both at headquarters and in each home. The tasks for headquarters are to plan ahead, set standards of service, design programmes for implementing change, monitor progress and to provide leadership. Leadership must be based on a positive vision of the role and purpose of residential child care which should be clearly articulated so as to strengthen and acknowledge the daily efforts of care staff. Staff experience at times severe difficulties; there is violence in units and many young people present great problems for adults to contend with; staff are frequently tested. The attitude of employers and managers towards care staff must show that they understand the difficulties of the task so that the attitude of staff towards those in their care can reflect a similar commitment and understanding. This is challenging and complex work.

Strategic Planning

5.3 Effective management to ensure good quality residential child care must be based on effective strategic planning. Residential child care services have to be positively framed within a strategic plan for child care services generally. The complex emotional, educational and health needs of the 2,000 or so young people and children admitted to residential child care homes in Scotland each year must be properly planned for and met in a consistent and appropriate manner.

5.4 Local authorities and other agencies invest a considerable amount of time and effort in drawing up plans for their child care services and some have also drawn up separate plans for residential child care. Several of these plans clearly articulate difficulties confronting residential child care provision. These include having wrongly located, wrongly sized or wrongly designed buildings; a lack of qualified staff; an increasing concentration of older young people and children with a multiplicity of difficulties and presenting significant challenges to staff; and a system generally ill equipped to provide adequately for identified needs.

5.5   A number of plans envisage considerable change in the nature of residential child care provision. The establishment of smaller sized units is a frequent theme as is the importance attached to increasing the numbers of qualified staff; the proportion varies. Some plans contain a clear strategic vision of how the authority considers residential child care should develop. In some cases the analysis and assumptions underlining that strategic vision are less clear.

5.6   For several of the plans there seem to be insufficient mechanisms or initiatives to ensure the involvement of other agencies with significant roles to play - in particular education, health, and voluntary organisations. In many authorities there are examples of good co-operation between social work and education in planning for children who are not in care. Plans are clearly and correctly aimed at minimising the risks of children coming into care (in many instances very successfully). For most authorities this co-operation seems less effective after the point at which children are received into care, when it is certainly as important and arguably is more important.

5.7   Admissions, often on an emergency basis, are a regular and dominant part of residential child care life and many homes find their attempts to provide stable care threatened by needing to handle unplanned, emergency and often inappropriate admissions. Too often homes designed to provide long-term care for adolescents after planned admissions have young people and children admitted as emergencies. Many have to care for children under 12 when this is outwith their stated function, and this causes added friction and distress for the young people and children as well as stress for staff.

5.8   Another significant factor is the high number of homes which find their mix of residents a significant problem. This is particularly the case in homes which do not provide education and in homes in the local authority sector. Heads of homes and others express much concern over the difficulties presented by mixing older and younger children within a unit. Such problems are endemic in residential child care today. They cannot be resolved without improvements in individual care planning, without better strategies for resource provision, without planned and controlled admissions or without a greater margin of available resources in order to reduce inappropriate placements.

5.9   A point which strongly emerges from the literature review is that to address issues about residential child care it is necessary to consider the integrated range of services for children, and a clear view of the contribution which residential care should make within that range. An unhelpful dichotomy between "community care" and "residential care" has developed. This can no longer be usefully sustained. It is clear that a great many young people and children who come into care will at some point be in residential care. Some estimates indicate that over 50% of young people in care over the age of 12 will spend some of their time in residential care. A commitment to cross existing boundaries is therefore an essential pre-requisite to ensure the development of effective care which focuses on the needs of the young person or child. As the National Foster Care Association pointed out in their submission to the review:

> "Placement decisions should ideally reflect the child's needs for either the experience of family life (available in foster care) or a more structured/specialised regime available in an identified residential establishment. It should not reflect a dewy-eyed optimism about the ability of one or other form of care to meet all children's needs. We are not being fair to children, nor are we being fair to over-stretched foster carers or residential workers, if we continue to play off one form of care to meet all children's needs".

5.10   For several authorities the current position appears to be that residential provision has diminished to the point where placement options realistically depend solely upon wherever there happens to be a vacancy. In such circumstances aspirations for individual care planning and good home management can seem a mere mockery. Agencies need to realistically plan the quantity and quality of residential child care needed or continue to pay a heavy price in the quality of care provided.

5.11 Because of their protection from immediate statutory responsibilities voluntary and private sector homes are well placed to control the number, nature and timing of admissions to their homes. Local authorities have to find other approaches to achieving a closer matching of needs and resources. It is local authorities who must plan what is required and specify standards. They must then consider what mix of provision will most effectively and efficiently meet those needs within available resources and how to purchase or make that provision.

5.12 There is no specific obligation on local authorities to produce plans for their child care services. There is no equivalent in this field to the requirements for community care plans or the strategic plans now required for social work services in the criminal justice system. A new planning system for child care services should be put in place in order to promote sound local planning and good collaboration.

5.13 Local authorities in Scotland vary considerably in size, in the problems they confront and in the opportunities they have. It is inevitable and right therefore that they should have different approaches to the provision of residential child care. Some plan to separate short and long-term admissions; others to reduce placement moves by linking homes to localities for most purposes. Whatever approach is chosen it must start from realistic analyses of the quality and type of care which will be required. A theme of the literature review and of the work of the review team is a constant interplay between "ought" and "is". For instance residential child care ought to be for over 12s only but in some areas is also having to provide for young children including under 5s. Strategic planning needs to firmly start from what is and find a path towards what ought to be. It must not be simply based upon what ought to be, leaving the front line staff to confront and deal with what actually is.

5.14 The essential elements in an effective planning process start from an evaluation of the strengths and weaknesses of present services, and an analysis of future demands and resources. They include clarification of objectives within an overall policy, and strategic choices on the most effective methods of achieving these objectives, translated into a plan which is clearly capable of implementation and which is widely communicated throughout the organisation.

5.15 Social work services for children and families operate within a network of other services, education and health in particular, and the responsible agencies must be carefully involved in the planning process if they are to aid the tasks of implementation.

5.16 Few if any authorities will be able to meet all of their needs themselves. Though it is understandable that each authority should wish to do so a realistic assessment needs to be made on the basis of considering the full range of requirements and how in practice these are to be best met.

> ***Recommendation 60: The Secretary of State should issue a direction requiring local authorities to produce and publish plans for social work services for children and families. These should include agreements between education and social work committees on collaboration in general and on how the educational needs of children in care are to be met and monitored; health boards and relevant voluntary organisations should also be consulted. Before the direction is issued the Social Work Services Group should consult with local authorities and other interests. The Group should subsequently issue guidance. The plans should include details of how the health, educational and social needs of children in local authority care are to be met.***

> ***Recommendation 61: The new local authority strategic plans for child care services should include a review of planned and emergency admissions to care, placement use and identified shortfalls. This should include a joint social work and education review of the use and provision of residential schools for young people and children with special needs.***

Recommendation 62: The statement of functions and objectives for each home should be clearly set within the framework of the authority's strategic plan.

Middle Management

5.17 Several authorities have increased and improved their middle-management support for residential homes and schools in recent years. This has allowed for better integration of the residential child care service with other aspects of child care provision and has been seen to be of benefit in this regard. It is important that middle managers have a good understanding of the homes tasks and functions and that they have a clear responsibility to ensure a high quality of care in the homes for which they are responsible, rather than simply a responsibility to allocate places.

5.18 Good planning, better training for officers-in-charge and more devolved authority should enable management improvements without increases in middle-management costs.

Leadership In The Home

5.19 The management tasks in the home are to translate plans and objectives into regular functioning of the home, to ensure staff are effectively deployed, briefed and trained and that the home is responsive to the individual needs of each young person or child. Together headquarters and home managers are key elements of the quality assurance system of residential child care.

5.20 The person in charge of any residential home has a pivotal role and exercises power well beyond their formal authority. The best set an example of good practice, support staff, young people and children and parents, maintain morale, keep an overview of developments, and represent the unit to the outside world. Officers-in-Charge must be able to manage the home as well as the staff and young people. Some officers-in-charge seem to lack authority even to order simple repairs or minor expenditures. Without this authority they cannot credibly hold the major responsibility for the well-being of the young people in the home.

5.21 In some homes officers-in-charge have the power to decide on admissions and the ability to help those who are ready to move on, to do so; in others the home seems rather the victim of decisions made elsewhere in relation to admission and discharge. Most of the time, the situation lies somewhere in between. Where the role of the home is not clearly defined and the officer-in-charge clear about their remit and authority, then effectively the needs of young people and children are taking second place. Maintaining the coherence of the unit requires clarity about the role of the Officer-in Charge. They cannot exercise proper leadership if they do not have sufficient organisational authority.

5.22 The management training of officers-in-charge is therefore of critical importance. Currently, officers-in-charge may find themselves holding a large budget with minimal training and no administrative support. For some authorities and agencies greater devolution of responsibility for a wide range of management and financial issues to officers-in-charge is required. This requires enhanced management training, time for the management task, and better administrative support. Management training is eligible expenditure for funding under the specific grant. The Scottish Office should finance and commission management training for officer-in-charge as a priority in 1992/93 and should consider, in due course, whether any further initiatives in relation to management training in social work services generally are required.

5.23 Officers-in-charge should have the authority to make flexible use of resources in order to use them effectively and efficiently and in order to provide a good quality service. It is wrong to trust someone to care for young people, but not to deploy small resources efficiently.

Recommendation 63: Officers in charge of residential children's homes should have delegated authority for budgets concerned with day to day running of the home including food, general supplies, decoration and minor repairs.

Managing for Quality

5.24 Some commentators have suggested that residential homes and other agencies should seek accreditation under BS5750 which is the standard specification for quality assurance schemes well established in industry and now being applied in some parts of the public sector including social work services. This standard for quality assurance systems comes complete with an external mechanism for verification. The process for working towards BS5750 accreditation may well be useful in helping an agency to think about the service it provides and how it measures success and that can help to engage and motivate front line staff.

5.25 However there are dangers in making the processes too elaborate. There is a danger of creating experts in quality assurance when what is needed is experts in residential child care. The real skill lies not in becoming "BS5750 experts" but in helping front line staff, managers and others to be interested in quality outcomes, to think in a structured way about what they are doing and to have confidence in their own and their agency's capacity for, and commitment to, continuous improvement.

5.26 Assuring quality can be described as three linked processes:

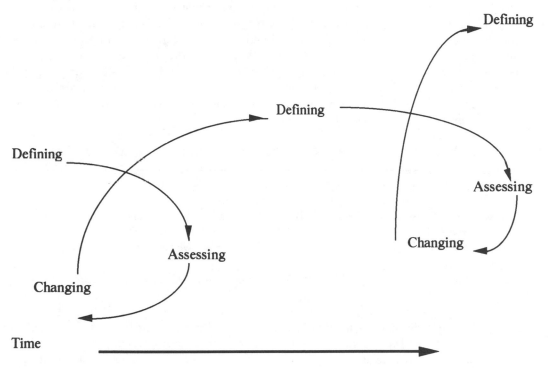

5.27 It is not always necessary to start at the beginning. Sometimes it makes sense to start by changing practice even before quality has been closely defined; but quality assurance means having all three stages operating in a co-ordinated way. In general the more responsibility there is for quality assurance at the point of service delivery, the more likely that real improvements in quality occur. At the same time people near the point of service delivery need a clear understanding of quality, of the overall process of service delivery and of their role within this.

5.28 The quality assurance system therefore needs to produce:

1. a working definition of quality for residential child care as a whole, and for component elements;

2. a continuous description of the match between quality as defined and residential care as provided; and

3. continuous action to align the provision of care with the definition of quality.

5.29 Defining quality for a particular unit has to happen within the framework of a Regional policy; and unit managers need active support from middle managers to interpret that policy and to develop a unit definition of quality. Members and senior managers should maintain a Regional policy that recognises and describes the role of residential care within the child care system.

5.30 If residential child care is seen only as a holding placement rather than as having a positive role to play then its quality will tend to be judged only on how well it assists the general child care system. Thus, it is possible to construct a definition of quality based on "the child care system" as a customer; such an approach would include standards in the form of statements such as "absorbs emergency admissions without fuss", "holds on to badly-placed children when we have failed to find better options". However this goes against the whole thrust of legislation and good practice, from the Social Work (Scotland) Act 1968 to the Citizen's Charter. It is essential that the young person or child should be regarded as the customer not the child care system and those who operate it.

5.31 Total quality management texts frequently refer to the "chain of customers" emphasising the point that everybody within the organisation is providing a service to an immediate customer, normally somebody else within the organisation and the quality of that internal service eventually determines the quality of the service to the external customer. The same is clearly true for residential child care. Everybody within local authorities or voluntary organisations who has anything to do with any aspect of residential child care - be they councillors, managers, residential staff, fieldworkers, personnel, supplies or education staff, - all affect the final quality of service provided to the young people and children. Children are not, however, straightforward "customers" of residential child care; they are also participants; they are part of the circle of relationships that constitute residential care.

5.32 Currently there is too little respect within that circle. Little respect for residential child care as a whole; little respect for young people and children in care; little respect for the staff of residential homes; little respect for the buildings or the issues of choice and supplies; and sometimes little respect from the young people and children of staff for the service they are offered. Without respect in the system the outcome cannot be a positive experience. It is not enough for residential child care staff, young people, children and their parents to be cared for and supported; for the system to work effectively they must be respected.

5.33 Lady Wagner's influential report Residential Care: A Positive Choice published in 1987 recommended that:

> "Every establishment - in statutory, voluntary and private sectors - should be required to draw up a staff training plan which should be subject to inspection procedures. The plan should be closely related to the aims and objectives of the establishment, and to its specific function and tasks."

5.34 It was anticipated that the plans would contain details of induction training, core training for all staff, training development and a system for regular appraisal of training needs. Though the Wagner report did not apply to Scotland it has been influential throughout the UK. Few homes or agencies, however, have been able to produce the kind of plans called for. Some very useful developments have taken place. The promotion of secondment schemes and the establishment of travelling coaching and training teams are examples that are well worth following. Overall however there remains a great deal to be achieved.

5.35 The Scottish Office has already issued a discussion paper on quality assurance[12] in social work services and further guidance will be developed in consultation with local authorities and other agencies. It is important that developments over the next few years should be clearly effective in the establishments. Improvements which can be achieved quickly are more important than planning for larger scale changes which may realistically take decades to achieve. The general approach should be to do what can be quickly done to enhance the quality of care, and pursue a policy of continuous improvement towards longer-term aims.

[12] "Improving Quality Assurance In Community Care" The Scottish Office 1991.

Recommendation 64: Local authorities and other agencies should extend their work on quality assurance to residential child care. The Social Work Services Inspectorate should monitor the development of quality assurance in residential child care between 1992 and 1996. In 1996 the Inspectorate should undertake a national inspection of residential child care. The report that inspection should also comment on the outcome of the recommendations in this report.

Inspection

5.36   Local social work authority inspection units were required from April 1992 to extend their functions to include residential child care. This change will mean that for the first time since 1968 the care provided in children's homes and schools will be regularly inspected. A regular inspection programme of residential child care is clearly essential to ensure the well being of young people and children in care.

5.37   Effective inspection depends on the development of appropriate standards to inspect against. The eight principles outlined in this report, and the recommendations, provide an initial framework within which the inspection units can conduct their work, but they need further development and adaptation. The establishment of standards and performance indicators is in any event an evolving process and inspection units should keep their work in this field under regular review. For any inspection it is essential that the views of some young people and children living in homes are obtained and also the views of parents. Such interviews must be conducted sensitively and arranged appropriately to the age and circumstances of the individuals.

5.38   Inspectors must also ask unexpected questions, they must probe discrepancies, look for information that may be being suppressed. Inspectors are not researchers. They should be wary of becoming so concerned with standards and performance indicators that they fail to keep their professional and human senses always alert. Systematic approaches to inspection are essential, but not in themselves complete. Analysis will miss some patterns that only become clear after calm reflection; moreover probing is essential, sometimes before the reason for it is clear.

5.39   Inspections require to be concerned with the way in which statutory requirements are met and with the adequacy of the buildings. They must pay careful attention to health and safety issues. They should also assess the home's performance on a qualitative basis and should examine what life in homes really means for the young people and children who are there. In this respect inspections will be helped by the publication of a "Charter for Children and Young People Living in Groups". This publication is a development of the Wagner Committee on Residential Care. It is expected that this Charter may be applied to all situations in which children are living in group care.

5.40   There is already adequate guidance material available in the field regarding standards of building design, record keeping, and staffing arrangements. It is important to develop more standards which reflect the experience young people and children have of care. The Scottish Office has already organised one seminar for local inspection units and consideration should be given to an annual seminar on inspection in residential child care. Local authorities have begun drawing up their own material on standards and indicators and it is important that this knowledge should be pooled across Scotland and that Scottish authorities are able to learn from developments elsewhere. Further guidance should be drawn up by the Social Work Services Inspectorate following consultation with local authorities, voluntary organisations and private agencies. (See Recommendation 7).

5.41   Arguments can be led both for and against local authority social work departments carrying responsibility for inspecting their own services. The independence of inspectors must be assessed in some form. Written submissions to the review commenting on this fell fairly equally between those in favour of local social work departments holding this responsibility and those who considered that greater independence from local social work departments was required. The government will be consulting further on arrangements for the inspection of social work services.

Recommendation 65: Local authority inspection procedures should always include some interviews with young people and children and their parents.

5.42   It is important to improve the knowledge base of social work, practice and policy. Inspection reports should contribute to general knowledge about residential child care. There will always be a need for more research, but there is also a need to give priority attention to the dissemination of research findings. SWSG has already commissioned a number of studies about aspects of residential care provision and in 1990 funded a major project on the development of integrated child care services which is due to be completed in 1994; the findings of this study should be widely disseminated.

5.43   Knowledge about the services, the new child care plans proposed in Chapter 5 and the national overview of these will depend heavily on the relevance, accuracy and speed of the statistical information available to planners and managers at local and national levels. A review of the statistical information systems should therefore go hand-in-hand with the consultation on planning guidance so that the best fit between the required statistical returns and the required plans is obtained.

Recommendation 66: In consulting about the content and form of plans for social work services for children and families Social Work Services Group should also consult about the statistical information system to inform these plans.

CHAPTER 6

Conclusion

6.1   Major developments in child care policy and practice have combined with population changes to alter dramatically the use made of residential care over the last two decades. No clear consensus has emerged about the role that residential child care should play within the new policies. The service has had to cope with rapid change without a clear sense of purpose, and staff, who are largely untrained, have felt that their work was not valued. This has resulted in persistent problems in providing a good quality of care, and sometimes crises regarding the care provided in some establishments. Nonetheless there are some establishments where excellent care has still been achieved, and probably every establishment can point to some successes.

6.2   Most of the written and oral evidence submitted to the review indicated widespread concern at the poor quality of care experienced by young people and children. The surveys conducted for the review, and the review team's visits, confirmed that there was serious cause for concern. In some children's homes, schools and units there are situations in which young people feel degraded, some homes are in a physical state of disrepair, many staff are unsure of their purpose, and most are untrained; too many youngsters do not know what plans there are for them, or where they are going; and youngsters, staff and parents feel largely powerless.

6.3   At the moment, despite examples of good practice, care and devotion, residential homes, and schools, often fail to provide the environment and circumstances suitable for young people who have suffered misfortune and for other reasons require and deserve extra care, support and, on occasion, control. The staff providing care feel undervalued and ill-equipped, and are not always doing a good job. Young people themselves feel they are not listened to and are subjected to regimes that do not meet their needs. Their parents lack confidence that substitute care is an improvement on their own and they feel they are unheard.

6.4   The reduction in the use of residential child care, though partly demographic, is a success story of Scottish social work. The increased use and support of family placements, and the effectiveness of measures to prevent reception into residential care are matters to take pride in. But residential child care is not just a residual service, the last resort when all else fails. It has positive roles to play and it must be enabled to play them well.

6.5   All young people and children need consistency in their care if they are to fulfil their potential. Inevitably young people in care experience considerable difficulties in this regard because of the changes in their circumstances. It is particularly important for them that there should be consistency in the care regime which they experience in any children's home or residential school, no matter how short or long a period they stay. This consistency is very hard to achieve under the current circumstances.

6.6   Staff training is the key to consistency in the way in which care is provided. The overall lack of appropriately trained staff in residential child care fits poorly with the task of undertaking some of the most challenging, complex and important work in social work services. The national training targets will not be easily or swiftly achieved. Induction and in-service training for all staff is equally important and progress in relation to these should be made immediately.

6.7   Training and the development of good practice is not easy in residential child care because of the obstacles to an inter-change of ideas and the spread of knowledge of best examples. The consultancy and development centre should assist this, but other initiatives at a local level are important. Managers must recognise the need for staff to exchange ideas and knowledge with those working in other authorities and agencies as well as within their own.

6.8   Good quality residential child care will always be needed for a small number of young people and children. Patterns of provision will continue to change. On the whole it seems likely to reduce further with the exception of a few specialist areas where it may expand, for instance, in providing respite or longer term care for young people who would otherwise be in hospital.

6.9   The quality of residential child care needs to be improved. No single group is to blame for the present position, however the responsibility for effecting change lies primarily with managers. The work of local inspection units is important and will assist. But quality cannot be inspected in; it can only be developed from a commitment at all levels to the continuous improvement of the service. That must spring from constantly listening to and responding to the experience of care provided to the young people, children and their parents.

List of Recommendations

be reviewed at least annually and the young people in the home should be assisted to contribute to this review.

9. Where locks are fitted to bedroom doors these should only be lockable from the outside and always be able to be opened from the inside. (Except for secure accommodation). Where bedrooms are shared, each young person or child should have a lockable cupboard or drawer. Young people and children should be able to make and receive telephone calls in private.   3.1.7 - 3.1.14

10. In homes and residential schools providing care for children and young people with complex social and educational needs accommodation should be designed or adapted to facilitate high quality care practices and access.   3.1.7 - 3.1.14

11. The Social Work Services Inspectorate after consultation, should issue practice guidance on providing residential care for young people and children who have been abused and those who abuse others.   3.1.19 - 3.1.22

12. In-service training for residential child care staff should include racial awareness training. Residential staff and managers should have training in anti-discriminatory practice.   3.1.23 - 3.1.25

13. Children with disabilities who require substitute home care but not treatment should be cared for in specialised residential or family provision and not in hospitals. Local authorities and health boards should develop their plans for the discharge of children in long-stay hospitals. The Scottish Office should consider an appropriate target date for the discharge of all children in long stay hospitals who do not require to be there.   3.1.26 - 3.1.31

14. The recommendations of the Child Care Law Review (Recommendations 23-25) which are concerned to extend the local authorities after-care responsibilities should be implemented as soon as resources allow.   3.1.36 - 3.1.43

15. The Social Work Services Inspectorate should evaluate "Looking After Children: Assessing Outcomes in Child Care" and issue practice guidance.   3.1.44 - 3.1.47

16. All agencies involved in residential child care should prepare a statement of rights and responsibilities of young people and children in care. This should cover key points in relation to the eight principles outlined in this report and include their rights to consult a general practitioner, and to complain confidentially; it should also outline their responsibilities in relation to behaviour and the specific rules of the home. Before (or at the latest on) admission to a home every young person or child should be given a copy of this statement. Such statements should be available in other language form (including Braille) when necessary.   3.2.2 - 3.2.9

17. All young people and children in residential care should be able to make a confidential complaint without the knowledge of the staff of the home. Parents of young people and children in residential care should similarly be able to make a complaint in confidence.   3.2.10 - 3.2.15

18. Complaints, allegations, or suspicions of physical or sexual abuse of young people or children in residential care, should always be referred to managers, or appointed agents out-with the home and its management; they should, in every instance where there is reasonable cause to believe that a child may have been the victim of abuse, inform the police. A record should be kept of any allegations made.   3.2.10 - 3.2.15

19. All young people and children in residential care should have the right to consider, with other young people and children, issues regarding the running of their home and to make suggestions and recommendations. Local authorities should consider instituting local procedural rights for young people and their parents to the effect that no review should be postponed without consulting them, and that they should be able to require that an overdue review be called.   3.2.16 - 3.2.22

20. Each local authority should consider supporting the development of "Who Cares" appropriate for its Region, and should ensure that all those in care can have access to it. The Scottish Office should consider the continued funding of "Who Cares" nationally, subject to a review every three years.   3.2.32 - 3.2.35

21. Greater priority should be given to the capital requirements for residential child care to accelerate replacement programmes.   3.3.1 - 3.3.10

22. Local authorities should set standards for the maintenance, repair and general furbishment of residential child care establishments (including standards for the time taken to effect repairs). Local authority inspection units should monitor the achievement of these standards in local authority and independent establishments.   3.3.1 - 3.3.10

23. Accommodation for young people with disabilities should be designed to ensure space for equipment and wheelchairs to be used in comfort.   3.3.1 - 3.3.10

24. Young people and children should always have access to simple food such as fruit, tea, juice, biscuits, bread, milk and cereal.   3.3.11 - 3.3.13

25. Formal purchasing arrangements involving the bulk buying of food and other domestic materials should be avoided.   3.3.11 - 3.3.13

26. Recreational budgets should always be sufficient to provide structured week-end and holiday activities.   3.3.18 - 3.3.21

27. Transport for residential child care establishments should not be marked in such a way as to distinguish it from an ordinary car or bus.   3.3.18 - 3.3.21

28. Local authority Education and Social Work Departments should review their arrangements for overseeing the educational needs of children in care, including those excluded from school. They should consider the designation of senior staff in both departments with responsibility to oversee the education of children in care.   3.4.1 - 3.4.17

29. Education and social work departments should ensure that arrangements are made for rapid exchange of documents and advice on the educational programmes and progress of the individual young people and children in order to prevent time being wasted in unnecessary educational reassessments.   3.4.1 - 3.4.17

30. Where the local authority have a responsibility or interest in the placement of a child in a residential educational establishment, that establishment should always be registered under Section 61(1) Social Work (Scotland) Act 1968.   3.4.18 - 3.4.21

31. Local authorities and health boards should review whether they have adequate liaison arrangements in place for overseeing the effectiveness with which the health needs of children in care are identified and met.   3.5.1 - 3.5.8

32. Local authorities and voluntary organisations should each have a clear policy on smoking and children in care. These policies should prohibit staff from smoking in residential homes (including field workers and other staff visiting residential homes); should prohibit staff (again all staff) from smoking in front of young people or offering young people cigarettes; and should clearly discourage smoking amongst young people, specifying limited rules and conditions under which young people are allowed to smoke. The policies should aim to establish a position in which homes and residential schools are smoke free environments for both staff and young people.   3.5.10 - 3.5.15

33. "Who Cares" should revise its statement to clearly discourage smoking and draw attention to young people's right not to be exposed to passive smoking.   3.5.10 - 3.5.15

34. All residential child care staff should have some training on sexuality and some key staff in adolescent units should be trained to take a lead role in ensuring that staff in the unit are confident in dealing with the complexities of the issues involved. The training should include training in relation to HIV/AIDS.   3.5.16 - 3.5.22

35. In-service training programmes should include elements that will assist care staff to feel competent and confident in working with young people experimenting with alcohol, drugs or solvents. Local authorities which have not done so should prepare practice guidance for care staff in relation to handling drug, alcohol and solvent abuse and appropriate information leaflets for young people in care.   3.5.23 - 3.5.25

36. Parents should be given a copy of the functions and objectives statement of the home before or when their child is admitted. They should be given an explanation of the general organisation and any house rules. They should be able to arrange a confidential discussion with their child (unless their is clear evidence that this would be detrimental for the child) and similarly with a member of staff. They should be kept informed of developments in their child's life.   3.6.1 - 3.6.5

37. Local authorities and agencies providing residential child care should draw up statements of rights and responsibilities for parents of young people in care. These should be issued to parents on or before admission of their child.   3.6.6 - 3.6.7

38. The formation of local and national organisations for parents of young people and children in care should be encouraged.   3.6.6 - 3.6.7

39. Local authorities should consider local joint training initiatives for education, social work, and other disciplines on collaboration in providing good quality residential child care.   3.7.1 - 3.7.4

40. Persons receiving allegations, or suspicious themselves, about possible abuse of young people or children in residential care should inform the police without hesitation.   3.8.4 - 3.8.5

41. The Social Work Services Inspectorate should convene a working group to draw up guidance on sanctions and control in residential child care. Once the guidance is issued Local Authority Inspection Units should review at least annually the adherence by each home to the guidance and should involve young people and children in this review. They should   3.8.17 - 3.8.27

also review staff training undertaken in respect of implementing the guidance.

42.	Statements of functions and objectives should differentiate clearly between (1) care provided, (2) sanctions and control permitted, and (3) any therapy available in the home. They should include details of any specialist training in therapeutic work.	3.8.17 - 3.8.27
43.	Local authority managers and Inspection Units should routinely gather information on absconding rates from residential homes and schools, and investigate patterns, causes and solutions based on the recommendations of the Absconding Working Party.	3.8.28 - 3.8.30
44.	The Scottish Office should review the future needs for secure accommodation following a national inspection in 1992/93 including an assessment of placements and use, distribution and condition of present provision and the quality of care provided. This review should also inform consideration of what further may be done to reduce the number of unruly certificates and also to avoid the imprisonment of young people of 16 or younger.	3.8.31 - 3.8.36
45.	In general, salaries and conditions of service of residential child care staff should be improved in order to attract and retain staff with sufficient ability and qualifications. Employers should recognise the range of skills required in different homes, and ensure that there is flexibility to determine salaries and conditions of service differentially.	4.2 - 4.5
46.	The Scottish Office should consider the applicability in Scotland of the recommendations of the Warner Inquiry into the selection and recruitment of staff in children's homes, and issue appropriate guidance in due course.	4.6 - 4.7
47.	Local authorities and independent organisations should aim to achieve a position in which 30% of all residential child care staff, and 90% of all senior residential child care staff hold a Diploma in Social Work or equivalent.	4.18 - 4.25
48.	Local authorities and independent organisations should aim to achieve a position, in which 60% of residential child care staff are assessed as competent at HNC/SVQ level 3.	4.18 - 4.25
49.	All students undertaking Diploma in Social Work courses should have at least one assessed group care placement.	4.18 - 4.25
50.	All residential child care staff should have 2 weeks induction training. This should be the training target given first priority.	4.26 - 4.30
51.	New staff with no previous experience of residential child care should be appointed on a probationary basis. Their appointment should be confirmed after one year only when assessed as competent at SVQ 2.	4.26 - 4.30
52.	Funding for voluntary organisations to second staff to qualifying training should be increased.	4.31
53.	Training consortia should consider the development of additional practice placements in residential child care, working to ensure that there are sufficient placements for the needs of their area. Funding should be made	4.32

available for additional practice placements in the voluntary sector, specialising in residential child care.

54.   The Scottish Office should fund additional social work lecturing resources   4.33
to be distributed across Scotland to promote the required expansion of
social work training.

55.   The Scottish Office should fund the establishment of a centre for   4.34 - 4.35
consultancy and development in residential child care. The specification
for the centre should be drawn up after consultation with relevant bodies.

56.   All residential child care staff should have regular supervision and agency   4.37 - 4.41
managers should initiate systems to monitor the provision of supervision.

57.   Qualified key workers should be able to hold full case responsibility within   4.43 - 4.44
agency review systems, when this is in the best interests of the young
person or child. When this is done, care should be taken to ensure that
young people and children continue to have regular contact with other
professional adults.

58.   Residential care staff should carry authority and budgetary responsibility for   4.45
individual expenditure to meet the basic care, recreational and
developmental needs of the young people and children in their care.

59.   The Scottish Office should finance and commission training material in   4.46
report writing for residential child care staff and teaching on the subject
should be included in training programmes.

60.   The Secretary of State should issue a direction requiring local authorities to   5.3 - 5.16
produce and publish plans for social work services for children and
families. These should include agreements between education and social
work committees on collaboration in general and on how the educational
needs of children in care are to be met and monitored; health boards and
relevant voluntary organisations should also be consulted. Before the
direction is issued the Social Work Services Group should consult with
local authorities and other interests. The Group should subsequently
issue guidance. The plans should include details of how the health,
educational and social needs of children in local authority care are to be
met.

61.   The new local authority strategic plans for child care services should include   5.3 - 5.16
a review of planned and emergency admissions to care, placement use
and identified short falls. This should include a joint social work and
education review of the use and provision of residential schools for young
people and children with special needs.

62.   The statement of functions and objectives for each home should be clearly   5.3 - 5.16
set within the framework of the authority's strategic plan.

63.   Officers in charge of residential children's homes should have delegated   5.19 - 5.23
authority for budgets concerned with day-to-day running of the home
including food, general supplies, decoration and minor repairs.

64.   Local authorities and other agencies should extend their work on quality   5.24 - 5.35
assurance to residential child care. The Social Work Services Inspectorate
should monitor the development of quality assurance in residential child
care between 1992 and 1996. In 1996 the Inspectorate should undertake
a national inspection of residential child care. The report of that

inspection should also comment on the outcome of the recommendations in this report.

65. Local authority inspection procedures should always include some interviews with some young people and children and their parents.   5.36 - 5.41

66. In consulting about the content and form of plans for social work services for children and families Social Work Services Group should also consult about the statistical information system to inform these plans.   5.42 - 5.43

Care Sanctions and Constraints: Draft Guidance for Consultation

The Social Work Services Inspectorate will convene a working group to review this draft guidance in the light of responses to its inclusion for consultation in this report.

A. INTRODUCTION

Guidance on sanctions and control for residential care of young people and children is inevitably difficult since it must endeavour to regulate matters which must often in some ways be individualised. Nevertheless it is essential that young people, their parents, staff and the public should know that these matters are appropriately regulated and not left simply to individual discretion. Only staff who genuinely like young people can use sanctions and controls appropriately and effectively in residential child care.

Many young people who are received into care have experienced troubled childhoods and disturbed relationships. Their needs are for security and stability, within a caring environment. As well as their need for care they, like all young people, also need to have clear limits set in order that they can experience security and develop self control. The child's age and stage of development must always be taken into account.

Sometimes the behaviour of young people will be unacceptable. In these circumstances it is important for staff to feel confident and supported in dealing with challenging and difficult behaviour. It may be necessary for staff to exert sanctions and controls, but it is essential that this is done in such a way that the respect for the young person, which is central to his or her care, is not compromised. It is the behaviour which is unacceptable, not the child.

Guidance and procedures are not a substitute for training. Training for residential workers must include the development of skills in setting clear limits for acceptable behaviour, the use of appropriate sanctions and controls and the management of conflict. Schedule 1 of the Residential Care Regulations 1987 requires that for each establishment there should be guidance on sanctions and constraints. Induction training, essential for all staff, should include training in the establishment's approach within the context of agency policy and guidelines; it should emphasise the importance of consistency in the staff team's approach and the value of creating an environment of mutual trust and respect; and it should include information on how staff can raise concerns about any inappropriate sanctions or controls they observe or suspect are being used by other staff. This induction training must be followed up with opportunities for development and review of skills and practice.

The power of the peer group in influencing behaviour is well documented and managing the peer group is a crucial skill for residential staff. Staff need to be adequately trained so that they can assist the group of young people to be mutually helpful, to minimise aggression and to ensure they do not provoke resistance and resentments.

B. WHY ARE CARE SANCTIONS AND CONTROLS NECESSARY?

To provide security for individuals and the group and to aid personal development. Young people need to develop an appreciation of the limits on their behaviour set by society and their community. They need to be helped to understand the implications of breaching these limits. A clear framework of authority (but not authoritarianism) facilitates the development of inner self-discipline and maturity. Children and young people need relationships where there is a reciprocity of responsibility rather than relationships based on power.

To protect the health and safety of others. It is unacceptable for a young person to act in such a dangerous way as to put others or him or her self at risk. Children and young people require to develop respect for self and others.

To maintain a positive homely environment. Wilful damage to property is unacceptable. It is detrimental to the quality of life of all the fellow residents and to the young person's own quality of life. Children and young people need to learn to value their own and other's property.

To maintain an emotionally positive and supportive atmosphere in the unit. Harmful and threatening behaviour to residents or staff by youngsters, or a member of staff, is unacceptable. Children and young people need to learn new ways of dealing with interpersonal conflict, anger and aggression.

All societies, groups and institutions require controls to regulate and order their activities for the benefit of the majority. Sanctions are found in every group, including families. Within residential care establishments sanctions should be measured and appropriate. They should not be used as a matter of routine, should be used sparingly, and their usage should be monitored and reviewed.

C. PERMITTED SANCTIONS AND CONTROLS

The following sanctions and controls are permissible when appropriately used.

1.   The restriction or withdrawal of privileges such as outings or leisure activities, including TV.

2.   The imposition of extra tasks, which must always be designed to be as positive and as productive as possible. These should be age appropriate and never beyond the capabilities of a child or young person.

3.   A child or young person may be separated from the group to a room on her or his own, as a means of enabling him or her to regain self-control. The door to the room must never be locked, and staff must monitor or accompany the child or young person throughout any period of separation.

4.   Where it is necessary to carry out (3) above and the young person refuses to comply it may be necessary to physically remove the young person. This is a serious matter and should never be carried out lightly. The force used should be the minimum necessary and care must be taken not to hurt the young person, restrict blood supply or breathing. Whenever possible this should be carried out with two members of staff present. (See E below.)

5.   It is appropriate for a young person or child to be fined sums from their pocket-money; rules regulating this should be clearly laid out in the statements of rights and responsibilities. The young person or child should never be deprived of more than three-quarters of his or her pocket money; fines may be extended over time.

6.   It is appropriate for a child or young person to contribute from his or her pocket money towards the cost of damages he or she has inflicted on property. Contributions may be collected over time and the limitation that no young person be deprived of more than three-quarters of their pocket money applies.

7.   Any article or substance belonging to a young person should be confiscated if it is considered to be potentially dangerous to self or others.

8.   Outdoor clothing may be withheld to reduce the likelihood of absconding. No young person, however, should be deprived of normal indoor clothing, or be required to wear alternative dress either as a form of punishment, or in order to prevent absconding.

9. Staff should express disapproval of unacceptable behaviour and make it clear that it is an obstacle to good relationships and to the peace and sense of safety which young people in residence have a right to expect.

D. CONTROLS WHICH ARE NOT PERMITTED

The following sanctions and controls should never be used.

1. No young person regardless of age should be subjected to any form of physical punishment, or the threat of physical punishment. No young person or child should be hit or smacked.

2. No young person should be deprived of any meal, nor should normal planned menus be modified or altered for the purposes of punishment.

3. No young person should be deprived of contact with any professional e.g. field social worker, lawyer, doctor.

4. Depriving a young person of contact with parents or adults with whom they have a significant relationship should never be used as a sanction; this includes, for instance, cancelling home leave.

5. Withdrawal of communication or positive engagement ("being sent to Coventry") should not be used.

6. No young person or child should be sent to bed early. This can be a more frightening and lonely experience than may be evident from the young person's behaviour. It is effectively unsupervised exclusion from the group and therefore carries potential dangers. Young people may be disallowed from staying up late to watch T.V. etc.

7. Withholding or use of medication, or medical or dental treatment, should not be used as a sanction.

8. Humiliation in any form should not be used.
   Only accommodation registered by the Secretary of State to provide secure care and a closed environment for children may use locked doors as a means of restricting a young person's liberty. Front doors of other establishments may be locked from the inside for security reasons as a normal home might be, and in order to protect very young children or children with serious learning difficulties. Bedroom doors which are locked from the outside and are not able to be opened from within are not permissible. Where a permitted sanction is exercised it should be recorded within the terms of the agency's procedures.

E. WHEN AND HOW TO USE PHYSICAL RESTRAINT

The concept of physical restraint involves securing the child's body so that it is not a danger to himself or to others. Physical restraint may be necessary in dangerous situations where there is serious risk to the child or young person's safety, or the safety of others. It may also be necessary in some situations which seriously threaten the stability of the group and the running of the home - this includes serious damage to property. Powerful and threatening young people can push other children into highly disruptive behaviour and should not be allowed to do so. Some, who have lacked early controls and security, have not developed effective controls of their sense of infantile omnipotence, causing them to be afraid of their own power and violence. They may push adults to the point of holding onto them until the fury has passed. Such feelings can be aroused in us all and should be prevented from spreading through the group.

Appropriate skilled use of physical restraint will include the development of a repertoire of methods, from requiring the child to confine him or herself in their room, to standing in the way of a child barring him or her from leaving, to physically taking hold of the child's person.

Where a young person or child requires to be physically held they should be offered a contract through dialogue offering assurances that the situation is safe, that they will not be hurt and that they will be helped to make the right choices.

Where physical restraint is necessary young people should be held by two adults, who should talk to each other, and continue to speak to the child about the choices. They should not engage with the young person's abusive conversation. The choices might take a form such as, "When you are quiet you will be asked to remain still for two minutes; then you will be permitted to sit for two minutes and finally to stand up and let us know you are able to take control of yourself." In this way the young person can come to understand that he or she is held safely until he or she resumes control of him or herself.

Young people who have developed violent responses to situations are afraid of their own violence and are looking for adults to take it from them. Using labels such as "bully, thug, violent" will exacerbate the problem. Other young people in residence also look to staff not to allow them to be bullied, terrified or abused by potentially violent residents. They need to see that staff are vigilant and very professional in their response to the violence of young people; that they do not get caught-up in the anger and violence, but have a carefully planned strategy, which is safe for all the young people and the staff.

The purpose of any physical restraint is to allow the young person, and others around him or her, to feel safe and secure and to demonstrate that bullying and violent behaviour are not tolerated. Account should always be taken of the child's age and stage of development when considering the appropriateness of different methods of sanction and restraint.

Children with learning difficulties may require a higher level of protection. If children do not understand or appreciate danger then staff have a duty to protect them and keep them safe. Restraints may include restricting access to certain rooms in the building. Such practices should be regularly reviewed and assessed to ensure they are necessary for safety. Restriction of liberty and restraint should never be used as a primary means of caring for children with learning disabilities whose development will depend on a stimulating environment with opportunities for exploring new experiences.

If physical restraint has been employed a senior officer must be briefed immediately regarding the circumstances. The incident should be recorded fully and parents and field social worker informed.

F. CONSISTENCY AND TRAINING

A clear understanding of, and commitment to, an agreed philosophy of care is essential. This should be reflected in the statements of functions and objectives. Informed by this the staff team must develop and maintain a consistent approach. This will reduce incidents arising and facilitate the effective handling of incidents that do arise. Consistency cannot be achieved without appropriate training, including induction training, nor maintained without regular review and staff development programmes. Guidance and procedures without training will prove of little value.

Following up after disruptive situations is crucial. It is important to help the child and staff understand what actually happened and why. Incidents should generally be followed up and discussed quickly, though the precise timing will need to be judged in the circumstances. Following-up incidents effectively helps to resolve the likelihood of them recurring.

Summary of the Literature Review

Andrew Kendrick and Sandy Fraser
Department of Social Work
Dundee University

The full Literature Review is published separately by The Scottish Office as a Research Paper

CONTENTS

1. INTRODUCTION

In studying the literature on residential child care we have identified 2 inter-related sets of problems. The first concerns whether it exists as a definable thing at all. There are different delineations and definitions of what constitutes residential child care and most authors find great difficulty in determining what is essential to it. The second set of problems concerns the relationship of what residential child care is in contrast to what residential child care ought to be. This is particularly evident in the debate about whether residential child care is (or ought to be) a last resort or whether it is (or ought to be) a positive choice.

We have placed certain limits on this review of the literature. We have accepted the distinction between foster care and residential child care and do not deal with the literature on foster care unless it directly impinges on the discussion of residential child care. Secondly, although residential child care could be taken to include educational establishments such as boarding schools and medical establishments such as hospitals, we have excluded these from the review.

2. DEFINITIONS OF 'RESIDENTIAL CHILD CARE'

Different authors, from various professional backgrounds, use different terminologies in relation to residential child care. This creates considerable difficulties in attempting to make these terminologies relate to each other.

Some authors, for example Seed and Thomson (1977), have pointed out how small the difference can be between foster care and the work of small children's homes. Beedell (1970) argued that foster care is a kind of residential care. However, he did not write about this 'type' of residential care in 'Residential Life with Children' because "foster parents do not, in general, take professional responsibility for their charges" (Beedell, 1970). For Jones, this very fact was used as the means to distinguish foster care from residential child care (Jones, 1979). By and large, fostering is seen as distinct from residential child care. Even where residential carers cater for very small groups of children which simulate the family and do not seem very different from foster placements.

If residential child care is, at its widest margins, care 'away from home' which is not foster care, is there anything else which can define it more precisely? Is residential child care a specific form of care?

It has long been recognised that the term covers a variety of care roles and lacks definition (Hey, 1973: Davis, 1981; Douglas, 1980; Jones, 1979; Tizard et al, 1975; Moss, 1975; Kahan, 1979; Payne, 1977). Nevertheless, an obvious concrete link between all forms of residential child care is that they provide overnight accommodation for their clients. Beyond this, in concrete detail and in operational assumptions they can differ markedly.

Jones uses the term residential social work to describe what occurs in a setting which acts as a substitute for a person's home. Within residential social work, he distinguishes 2 forms of social action: firstly, 'daily routines', and secondly, 'social work services'. If these 2 forms of social action are fully integrated, then the establishment can be described as a 'therapeutic community'. The residential care setting is distinguished from other forms of care in terms of: (a) its level of planned integration of social work services and daily routines and; (b) its lack of spontaneity and immediacy, said to be a feature of family life (Jones, 1979).

Barker makes a distinction between 'residential treatment' and 'residential care'. He argues that 'residential treatment' should not be confused with 'residential care' and that it is important to distinguish between the care given in foster homes, group homes, detention units and other places where children are looked after away from their families and the therapy provided in treatment centres (Barker, 1988).

Within the sphere of residential treatment another distinction has been made. This is between the 'therapeutic milieu' and 'milieu therapy' (Mayer et al, 1978). Basically, 'therapeutic milieu' refers to a particular kind of setting in which treatment occurs whereas 'milieu therapy' refers to a technique of treatment. In the 'therapeutic milieu', the objective is to create a community in itself. It is the intention of the 'therapeutic milieu' that a child should experience social life in a way which is distinct and separate from normal community life. 'Milieu therapy', however, may be followed by establishments which do not subscribe to this totalising view. In this situation, the institution acts as 'mediator' between the community or family and the child. The important point which distinguishes 'milieu therapy' from other forms of therapy used in social work is that it is conducted in a group context. Part of the package of care has to include a belief that the child will benefit from the group-living experience. In 'mediatory institutions', the degree of control over the treatment environment by staff is substantially limited by the extent of permeability to the community-at-large (Mayer et al, 1978).

The term 'residential child care' can be seen as an enveloping concept which contains both 'care' and 'treatment'. There is a general tendency to view both terms as relating to methods of dealing with particular social problems. This is alluded to by Ward when she offers another view of 'residential child care'. She explains, as does Payne (1977) and Jones (1979), that residential care is 'social work', but differs from other forms of social work in so far as "social work in a residential setting is about working with people in a shared day-to-day living experience (Ward, 1980, p.25). This necessarily includes an understanding that 'relationships as they happen' can occur in a spontaneous way with a high degree of 'immediacy' (cf. Jones, 1979, above). These relationships are defined as operating at 2 levels, first, at the level of the person/child and his/her 'personal states and processes' and second, in relation to the person and his/her outside world (Ward, 1980).

Ward portrays a range of 'residential care' and she argues that regimes which 'punish', exemplified by 19th century Poor Law Institutions, tend to deny the responsibility of social conditions for social and individual actions. However, she also points out that even under today's more liberal climate "... we are still assigning the institution the task of 'doing something with' those people who are failing to cope in the community. Being unable to cope burdens other people with unwanted pressure, so the burden is transferred to the institution. Thus the institution is assigned a double function; to provide care for its inmates and to provide space for unwanted feelings of the parent society" (Ward, 1980).

Many advocates and opponents of residential child care remain fixed in their conception and definition of residential care as a segregated environment (Lee and Pithers, 1980). An attempt to move away from such a definition of residential child care which separates an 'institutional care element' from a 'community care element' is to be found in Ainsworth and Fulcher (1981). The significant feature of residential care, it is argued, is the group-living experience. This feature links residential child care to other forms of community-based group care (for example, day-care, family-centres, and Intermediate Treatment groups). It attempts to distance residential child care from antecedents suggestive of uncaring, deterrent or socially isolating regimes.

The potential of this definition of residential child care as 'group care', is that it could conceptually unify a continuum of service from community-based non-residential provision to residential provision. In doing this, the authors implicitly set up another continuum of service which does not relate to groups; what might be called a continuum of individualised-care services. Constructing residential child care in this way has the potential advantage of integrating 'group care' provision within community-based provision. There are problems in this however. The criticism of the concept of 'residential child care' being imprecise can be made for 'group care' too. A range of quite different 'care' or 'treatment' programs can be found within 'group care'. Some of these may be concerned with how the child relates to parents and the community; others may be more concerned with individualising social problems. Such a range is referred to in Whitaker's contribution to Ainsworth and Fulcher's book (Whitaker, 1981).

A different delineation of residential child care is presented by Davis (1981). She concludes that all forms of residential care fall into one of three categories. Family-substitute care, attempts to be a substitute on a long or short-term basis for 'normal family life', more or less by simulating an ideal version of 'the family'. Examples of this can be found in the family group home widely established after the Curtis Committee report of 1946. Family-alternative care attempts, on a long or short term basis to create an alternative to 'normal family life', for example, a hospital ward, or a therapeutic community. Family-supplementary care, neither attempts to substitute or be an alternative to 'normal family life': rather, residential care is used to support and sustain children and families who face varying types of crisis. Usually this is seen as short-term work, although, in fact, the term need not exclude long-term work with families (Davis, 1981).

These divergent views of residential child care illustrate the problems of definition. This is further compounded by the problems of categorising the empirical reality. Parker stated that it is difficult to estimate the exact extent of residential child care (Parker, 1988b). He divides residential child care, into numerous categories: residential nurseries; ordinary children's homes; observation and assessment centres; Community Homes with Education (former approved schools); private children's homes; boarding special schools and LEA boarding schools; and penal establishments.

If we look at residential care even within the category of 'children's homes', the picture is, in fact, complex. This group of establishments is significant because it accommodates twice as many children as do all other forms. However, within these children's homes there are differences of approach (Berridge, 1985).

Berridge indicates the problems in developing a classification of children's homes. He states that in practice "it proved difficult to classify homes in terms of their child care tasks. There were many inconsistencies and factors which did not go together" (Berridge, 1985). He settled on 2 'administrative criteria' as the basis of his classification, the size of the home and leadership style, although he pointed out that there was a "serious mismatch between these and other important social work dimensions" (Berridge, 1985).

On this basis, 3 styles of children's home were identified. The 'family group approach', small units, where the head of home is the main provider of pastoral care and who has management responsibility for the home. The 'hostel model', of medium size, headed by an officer-in-charge who is involved in everyday affairs, but who works as part of a wider staff group. The 'multi-purpose homes', in which "the head of home occupies the role of director and co-ordinator and has only limited involvement in the daily care of children" (Berridge, 1985). Berridge makes the significant point that these characterisations are not based on any appreciation of children's needs or rights.

The term "residential child care', then applies to so wide a field and to such diverse elements that determining what it is in a positive sense is more or less impossible. 'Residential child care' is an englobalising term. In attempting to make the complex simple, the term 'residential child care' undermines awareness of the significant differences between establishments which care for persons away from home. It is important to focus more directly on specific types of residential provision and examine their strengths and weaknesses.

3. THE SCOTTISH CONTEXT: RESEARCH ON RESIDENTIAL CHILD CARE IN SCOTLAND

Over the past 15 years residential provision for children in care in Scotland has fallen dramatically from 6,336 in 1976 to 2,364 in 1989. The number of residential establishments fell from 288 to 163 over the same period. This reflects the change in social work department placement policy which emphasises placing children at home or in community placements rather than in residential establishments. Whereas 36 per cent of children in local authority care were placed in residential establishments in 1976, this had fallen to 20 per cent in 1989.

This has been accompanied by a change in the role of residential placements. In 1977, one-third of children in care under the age of 5 were in residential establishments but by 1989 less than one in 20 were. For children in care between 5 and 12 years of age the fall was also dramatic from just under one-half to less than one in 12. However, for young people aged 12 and over there was only a very small reduction from 34 per cent to 30 per cent. This has meant that in 1989 the vast majority of children in residential care (86 per cent) were aged between 12 and 17.

There are 2 principal routes to placement within residential schools: through the Children's Hearing System and through the courts. Bruce reported that in 1973 this double track system resulted in one in 5 child offenders being referred to the procurator fiscal, and one in 11 being prosecuted in the sheriff court (Bruce, 1982).

In the 1970s, Rushforth conducted research to see if there were differences in the background of children placed in List D schools by the Children's Hearings and the courts and whether they responded to training in the List D schools differently. She found no statistically significant differences in the family background of the 2 groups nor in the background of offending prior to committable offences. Only 4 percent had been sent to court because of the seriousness of the offence whereas almost two-thirds of the court sample were co-accused with an adult. There was a good deal of regional variation in terms of referral through courts and children's hearings. Children referred through the courts were more likely to remain in custody prior to placement; to wait longer for a place; and to wait for a place in a penal establishment, rather than at home (Rushforth, 1978).

Rushforth studied a limited set of 'responses to training': absconding, re-offending, corporal punishment, length of stay in the school and destination on departure from the school. The only significant difference between the 2 groups of boys was to do with absconding and this related to the pattern of absconding rather than the overall level of absconding, a higher percentage of panel than court boys had absconded 3 times or more (Rushforth, 1978).

When Rushforth interviewed staff in List D schools she found that few of them clearly understood the rationale behind court appearances and a number of them clearly felt that these boys must be more serious offenders. There were also clear discrepancies between staff perceptions of concepts of control, punishment and treatment and their views of the children's hearings orientation in relation to these concepts. She comments that contradictions and ambiguities were apparent in perceptions about the welfare/treatment and criminal justice models which partly result from the dual track system.

In 1987, the Lord Advocate revised the categories of offences which are to be reported to procurators fiscal concerning the appearance of children in the court system (Kearney, 1987). This has led to a reduction of children being tried in courts.

Martin, Fox and Murray's study of the Children's Hearing system focused on decision-making. The number of times that a child had previously appeared before a hearing was associated with the decision reached. Of those children who had never appeared before a Hearing before, only 4 per cent were placed in a residential establishment whereas 32 per cent were placed in a residential establishment when they had 4 or more previous appearances before the Hearing. They comment that residential supervision remains a minority disposal even for the most hardened recidivists. The authors looked at the factors which affected Panel decisions. Whilst they argue that supervision decisions at first or second hearings "can be predicted with a high degree of accuracy", this did not hold for decisions about residential supervision. They came to the conclusion that in general the decision to place children in residential placements involves a larger element of idiosyncratic judgement than the less weighty decision to bring a child under the supervision of a social worker (Martin et al, 1981).

Two studies have looked at secure accommodation in Scotland (Petrie, 1980; Kelly and Littlewood, 1983, 1985a, 1985b, Littlewood, 1987, Littlewood and Kelly, 1986). In 1984, there were 3 secure units in Scotland attached to List D schools providing 67 secure places. As well as the secure units a number of List D schools had 'custody' rooms and cells and assessment centres also have secure facilities within the establishment. Stewart and Tutt have noted the dramatic increase in secure accommodation in relation to open provision. In the 1960s, there was a ratio of 1 secure bed to 68 open beds; by 1984, the ratio was 1 to 10 (Stewart and Tutt, 1987).

Discussing the figures for Great Britain and Ireland as a whole, Stewart and Tutt found that 73 per cent of the under-17s who were in penal institutions had previously been removed from their families, most commonly into residential child care. More than half had been previously placed in an open assessment centre, two-fifths had been placed in children's homes and nearly a half had been placed in open Community Homes with Education, List D schools or their equivalent (Stewart and Tutt, 1987).

The studies by Petrie, and Littlewood and Kelly found that there was some reason to question the process of assessment for placement in secure accommodation. Petrie studied 2 groups of 100 boys placed in a List D school and the attached secure unit. Fifty-nine Percent of boys in the secure unit were sentenced through the courts compared to 33 per cent of the school boys and 64 per cent of school boys were from Hearings as opposed to 34 per cent of the secure unit boys. However, Petrie found that the offence histories of the boys in the 2 groups were similar and the main difference lay in the fact that those in secure accommodation had persistently absconded from previous placements and had significantly more placements. A larger number of boys who had committed offences of violence were in the open school rather than the secure unit. The family circumstance of the 2 groups of boys were also very similar. Petrie's conclusions on the reasons why boys are placed in secure accommodation are important and she states that "it is because the boys have persistently refused to stay in open institutions. It is not because they are more dangerous". (Petrie, 1980)

Littlewood and Kelly compared 2 groups of children referred to a secure unit: those placed in the unit, and those turned down by the referral group. Few children constituted a serious risk to others. Most frequently children were referred for absconding, glue sniffing or for offences such as theft, shoplifting or housebreaking (Kelly and Littlewood 1983). When both groups were compared in terms of reasons for referrals, they were found to be indistinguishable. Littlewood and Kelly conclude that placement in the secure unit was an arbitrary decision and was more likely to be due to extraneous factors rather than the child's behaviour (Kelly and Littlewood, 1985a). The Scottish research confirms other findings that the demand for security reflects the requirements of inadequate, open institutions and community services rather than the needs of difficult children (Millham et al, 1978; Cawson and Martell, 1979).

The Scottish research of List D schools and secure accommodation has also questioned the process of residential intervention. Walter's study of a List D school focused on how the perceptions of the boys placed in the school fitted into the treatment-based philosophy of the school. Walter found that the boys' main concern was in terms of 'getting out' and that this is reflected in the boys' major concern with good behaviour which they see as the means of release. However, Walter argues that the boys do not define fears and anxieties about home or school as relevant to release. The manner in which boys discussed this led Walter to conclude that they felt it inappropriate to talk in public about things awry in one's family. This inhibits the production of the kind of information staff need to diagnose their 'problems'. This led, in Walter's view, to different agendas being placed on meetings which were formally to deal with boys' problems (Walter, 1978).

Achieving release from the school, Walter found, was based on 2 main criteria; having been in the school for at least 6 months (a throw back to the approved school system); and having achieved 'grade 5'. Each month boys were 'assessed' but Walter comments that going up a grade each month routinely depends on the boys behaving well, not on whether their personal problems are being solved. There was limited contact with field social workers or with the boys' families while they were at the school and he concludes that in the absence of adequate information from outside, staff have only the boys' behaviour within the school to go on. Walter concluded that Dalmore staff were limited in the degree to which they were able to make the official philosophy of treatment of individual 'problems' anything more than rhetoric (Walter, 1978).

In their study, Littlewood and Kelly found that while staff maintained a commitment to concepts of treatment and rejected concepts of custody in an idealistic sense, they gave them equal weight in terms of the situation on the ground in the secure unit (Kelly and Littlewood, 1985b). Most of the staff considered that there was no formal programme of treatment being undertaken and there was no evidence of any particular treatment model in operation. While each child in the unit was appointed a key worker, there was limited use of this relationship in terms of individual treatment due to lack of staff expertise and lack of management commitment to individual treatment objectives. The assessment of the progress of children was, to a large degree, based on intuition and common sense (Littlewood and Kelly, 1985b).

There was also ambiguity and conflict around the issue of control. The unit used no formal incentives other than the loss of leave or release as a deterrent. However, there was little physical violence in the unit, and staff considered there to be little difference between the children in the unit and those in the open schools. The children interviewed in the study generally did not consider punishment as the Unit's aim and staff were for the most part viewed positively. They stressed conformity both in terms of staff expectations of them and as a means to their release (Kelly and Littlewood, 1985b).

Littlewood and Kelly followed up a group of young people following their release although, due to problems in keeping track of young people, the authors stress that the group was not representative. The process of release was considered by the authors as important. Release breaks all formal contact with the unit and the majority of the interviewed children felt ambivalent, sad, frightened or angry on the day of release. Nearly all the young people had become criminally involved again and few had been able to find work on their own behalf. The authors made 2 basic recommendations from their follow-up study. The first concerned the lack of priority placed on education in the unit and the importance of at least attempting to provide young people with work-relevant scholastic or vocational credentials. The second stressed the finding of the complete break at release and the importance of the need for secure unit staff to follow-up the young people after release. (Littlewood and Kelly, 1986).

Petrie followed up the cohort of boys by questionnaire to their social worker. Seventy boys from the secure unit and 53 boys from the open school ended up in custody following release and Petrie concludes that the levels of re-offending present a gloomy picture and "deepen the impression that both sets of boys have passed through a 'criminogenic experience'" (Petrie, 1980, p. 135). Petrie also stresses the importance of support in the period following release.

The research by Petrie, Littlewood and Kelly indicates and implicitly questions the effectiveness of residential placement in terms of recidivism. This point has also been made in relation to the English context in a comparison of 2 treatment approaches in Knighthood Training School (Cornish and Clark, 1975). Thornton et al (1984) came to similar conclusions when they studied the tougher regimes introduced into detention centres and showed that there was no discernible effect on reconviction rates.

While treatment or training programmes may be successful in modifying behaviour and attitudes, it seems that this modification is contextually situated and cannot be prolonged once the offender leaves that setting. The long-term ineffectiveness of such residential programmes for juvenile offenders is an important argument for intensive community support and intermediate treatment programmes (Thorpe et al, 1980; Bilton and Thorpe, 1987).

In relation to assessments and decision-making about residential child care, Ford suggests that there is a need to know what the intentions and expectations of panel members are, and equally a need to understand the realities of the situations that the children who are sent to these establishments will actually encounter. However, she concluded that very little information was available (Ford, 1982). The situation has changed little in the 10 years since she wrote this.

4. RESIDENTIAL CHILD CARE IN THE CONTEXT OF COMMUNITY-BASED SERVICES

In discussing residential child care in relation to community-based provision, one has to be aware of the fact that the term 'community' is problematic in its own right and carries with it historical and ideological overtones and baggage. There is one important distinction which needs to be made between the community in which a residential establishment is located and the child's home community. These may be the same but are not necessarily so. The importance of this distinction can be seen when residential care is contrasted with foster care which is frequently represented as community care provision. Indeed some types of foster parents in Scottish Social Work Departments are called 'community carers'. However, community carers often do not live in the child's own community and there are important issues about the effects of rurally-based foster parents caring for children from city environments.

In family-substitute homes, discussion of the relationship of residential homes with the community, for the most part, relates to the neighbourhood in which is is situated. White, for example, in discussing Mill Grove children's home argues that in the long-term care of children the application of specific treatment models - 'educational', 'therapeutic', or 'behavioural' - are inappropriate. He defines Mill Grove as operating a 'family' or 'organic' model (White, 1979). One of the requirements for admission to Mill Grove was an 'irretrievable breakdown between child and parents. The relationships of Mill Grove with the community are concerned almost totally with its surrounding locality and there was a commitment to make facilities available to neighbours and local organisations. In the family-substitute home, this is the child's home community. Pick (1981) describes very similar relationships with the local community.

In his study of children's homes, Berridge described family-substitute homes as family group homes. They are designed to merge with their surrounding environment and children are generally unrestricted in their movements. Berridge describes the staffing of the homes as matriarchal and the head of home assumes responsibility for daily management, pastoral care and contact with field workers. Berridge noted that the homes were preoccupied with 'secondary' rather than 'primary problems' - with problems generated by the residential experience, rather than with the factors which brought about the child living away from home (Berridge, 1985).

Kelsall and McCullough (1988) discuss the changing role of residential child care away from the family-substitute model towards the family-supplement model. They stress the need to develop purposeful, systematic and flexible work with families. In discussing one children's home, Gray's Hill, they identify some of the problems involved in this. They point to the difficulties for children in residential care in keeping in contact with their families and this has been highlighted by Millham et al (1986). If children do keep in contact, Kelsall and McCullough argue that residential staff are not confident in undertaking family work, partly because of their lack of qualifications. Staffing levels and shift systems also interfere with attempts to deploy staff outwith the children's home. Family work depends almost entirely on families visiting the children's home but this was never particularly encouraged by residential or fieldwork staff. Residential staff had little autonomy and while they used a key-worker system, there was ambiguity about the boundaries between their role and the fieldworkers (Kelsall and McCullough, 1988).

The same situation was found in relation to 'after care'. Gray's Hill staff could be allocated to children staying independently in the community but if there were problems, the fieldworker would take over responsibility for the case. If the child returned home, then responsibility would immediately pass back to the fieldworker. Kelsall and McCullough question the wisdom of this and argue that residential staff have a role to play in supporting children when they have returned home. Fraser similarly describes a children's home where the explicit aims of residential staff working with the children's' families were bedevilled by the resource implications of such work (Fraser, 1989).

Baldwin elaborates the various ways in which the usage of the children's homes undermines the social work intervention of the residential staff involved and uses this evidence to argue that residential child care ought to be used within an integrated range of child care services (Baldwin, 1990). One example of this and the difficulties involved is given in Stewart, Yea and Brown (1989).

The study contrasts 2 divisions of a social services department undergoing a fundamental change of social work policy where the aim was to transfer resources out of the long-term residential sector into community based preventative services and alternatives to residential care. Family Centres provided a local focus for child care services and facilitated the co-ordination of several aspects of a continuum of child care services such as assessment, short and long-term residential care, foster care and preventative activities including day care, domiciliary support and Intermediate Treatment (Stewart, Yea and Brown, 1989). An important element of the policy was that residential and fieldwork staff should work together more closely and more flexibly. To encourage such co-operation the functional split between residential and day care and fieldwork services was removed and the management of the Family Centres became the responsibility of the local fieldwork Manager.

The study focused on the professional issues and attitudinal changes associated with this closer co-operation of residential and fieldwork staff. The authors concluded that the lack of change they found, confirmed the lasting effect that traditional role sets have on work identity and the consequent difficulty of changing mutual expectations. The 2 divisions, however, showed contrasting results and while progress was observed in the relationship between fieldworkers and residential workers in one division, there was a marked lack of change in the other division. These differences indicate that integration of residential and fieldwork services does not simply depend on structural change in the organisation and highlights the importance of external management in promoting change (Stewart, Yea and Brown, 1989).

The practical problems of developing community-based residential provision have also been highlighted in 2 studies, Dharamsi et al's account of the Harlesden Community Project (1979) and Cox and McArdle's evaluation of Druid's Heath (1986). Dharamsi et al indicate that there was a considerable degree of tension in relations between project workers and field social work staff particularly in relation to decisions about which children to admit to the residential home

(Dharamsi et al, 1979). In relation to the local community, control problems within and outside the building which housed the Harlesden project, provoked a reaction which ultimately closed the project. The consequences, then, in citing children's homes in urban areas generally and in inner city areas in particular, must be considered carefully. There is no place for naivety about the supposedly beneficial affects of placing children close to their own 'community'. The Harlesden Community Project workers stressed the importance of taking into account the resource and support implications for work in a children's home in a disadvantaged community (Dharamsi et al, 1979).

Druid's Heath was based on a federation of children's units: General Support Units (GSUs) which were dispersed community based living units with linked foster homes; and centrally located units concerned with education, 'alternative care', family placement and general administration (Cox and McArdle, 1986). Initially, difficulties in recruitment and tensions between social work and education staff contributed to problems in caring for young people who were admitted because they were among 'the most difficult'. Also the absence of key components of the structure such as the alternative care unit meant that the open community-based units had to deal with episodes of difficult behaviour for which they were not designed but with no alternative resource to call on (Cox and McArdle, 1986).

The federal nature of the structure created further problems. To work it had to have a good internal communication network but the geographical spread of the units frustrated this objective. Moreover, budgets for transport, telephones and staff time were underestimated. There was conflict between the demands of individual units and the development of the organisation as a whole. Further, workers in different units did not present a coherent set of care and treatment principles (Cox and McArdle, 1986).

These internal problems of development existed simultaneously with problems in relation to the external environment. When the Centre was planned 5 different local authorities supported the federal idea. However, different local authority policies meant that only 2 consistently used Druid's Heath. Demand for places never reached the level envisaged in the planning stage and because the Centre was used as a 'last resort' by some authorities, more difficult children were admitted which inhibited more general and preventive work in the local area. Some young people also had to be placed in GSUs at some distance from their home area and staff had to spend time and resources in creating ways for these people to return home for weekends or other purposes. The structural base for work with the family, the local community and local social workers was therefore not sound. While Cox and McArdle concluded that Druid's Heath practice in relation to parents might have been in advance of other CHE's, the involvement of staff and parents in the general care of children was still very limited. The raison d'etre of the whole Druid's Heath Centre seemed to be undermined by its structural failures. It could not do the job it was designed to do (Cox and McArdle, 1986).

If the role of residential child care in the community is to be part of the process of social work engagement with families in that community, then there are signs of response to this aim. However, there are also problems with this response. Residential child care is also to change. At the heart of the slow pace of change there are both resource issues and ideological issues. Ideas need to change in order that more resources can flow towards adequate staffing and adequate training for a more extensive and engaging role. Received wisdom has suggested that residential care based on the family model has been inadequate in terms of contact with the child's family and surrounding community. But examples of 'multipurpose homes' or 'family-supplementary homes' have not shown that it has been any easier to establish appropriate relationships with family or community. In most of these studies, issues of inadequate staffing levels and inadequate training have not permitted planned levels of work. Stewart, Yee and Brown (1989) have shown that the required attitude shifts of staff and management are also problematic.

5. RESIDENTIAL CHILD CARE: LAST RESORT OR POSITIVE CHOICE

The most significant link between all forms of residential care in this country is that, in an ideological and historical sense, they share roots either in the Poor Law of 1834 or in reactions to it (Davis, 1981; Parker, 1988a; Fraser, 1989). Institutions providing residential care necessarily involved reactions to perceived social problems, rather than to the expressed needs or rights of individuals. Residential child care, whether this took the form of hospitalisation, entrance into the workhouse or voluntary children's homes involved segregation, containment and surveillance. There has been a continuation of segregated environments which have been called, as a generic term, residential child care. In these circumstances, residential care has been used as a 'last resort', because it has involved a substantial move away from families (Davis, A. 1981; Rasmussen, 1984).

This viewpoint has been substantiated by the work done which has highlighted the negative aspects of residential child care and the stigma attached to it. Berry concluded from a study of 44 residential establishments that a sizeable proportion of children have a comparatively poor experience of daily care in residential life (Berry, 1985). The problems associated with living in residential establishments have included the instability of the care due to the high turnover of staff. A further criticism of residential care has concerned the lack of privacy of residents, in part due to cramped conditions, the sharing of bedrooms, chests and wardrobes, and the lack of space for access visits (Knapp and Smith, 1984; Newman and Mackintosh, 1975; DHSS, 1986b).

Triseliotis and Russell's comparative study of outcomes of adoption and residential care highlighted the negative images of care held by those who had been in residential placements. The experience was felt to have ruined their childhood. Feelings of isolation and stigmatisation were particularly stressed (Triseliotis and Russell, 1984). The young people in the 'Who Cares' survey also graphically describe the stigma attached to living in residential care (Page and Clarke, 1977).

Set against these criticisms is the argument that there is a role for residential child care as an integrated element of a continuum of care provision. In a comprehensive review of residential care, Wagner argues that within the continuum of care provision, clients must be allowed 'real and valid alternatives'. That is, the child must perceive his/her needs and then have the right to act and access the form of care which he/she positively wishes. Therefore, within the continuum of care provision, admission to residential care "... should not necessarily be seen as a mark of failure either on the part of the family or of those working in support of them" (Wagner, 1988). The 'positive choice of residential child care' should be associated with "the positive aim of providing care away from the family home as a means of providing support to the family and preventing the risk of long-term family breakdown" (Wagner, 1988, p. 96). That is to say, residential child care should have a common goal with other parts of the social work provision of preventing family breakdown. However, it should also be capable of offering a positive choice to children of an alternative to family life as part of a continuum of care provision (Wagner, 1988).

The contradictions inherent in this formulation are not adequately dealt with in the Wagner Report. The affirmation of the family (however defined) has always been previously linked to a policy of 'last resort' for residential child care. This, linked to the serious failings of residential establishments in the past and present diminishes, to a large degree, the use of residential child care as a 'positive choice'. The question of the compulsory use residential care also must be taken into account when discussing the role of young people in having a 'positive choice' (Packman et al, 1986; Waterhouse 1988a).

Nevertheless Wagner suggests 5 areas where there is a continuing need for residential child care provision in terms of providing for a 'positive choice': respite care where there is planned or emergency relief for families and children; preparation for permanent placement where residential care can provide planned support towards permanency especially where children have experienced repeated breakdowns in previous placements or home situation; the keeping of families together both in terms of sibling groups being in care together and in terms of continuing contacts with parents and other relatives; care and control for the small minority of disturbed children who require specialist secure provision; and therapeutic provision for socially and emotionally damaged children (Wagner, 1988).

However, as Wagner acknowledges, often the element of choice which is expressed above is not present and the "... admission of children to residential care is too often the result of a crisis or a failure of planning; this has led to residential care becoming a residential resource instead of providing the necessary element of choice among a range of other services" (Wagner, 1988).

Thus, older themes and traditions within residential child care may be easily reinforced and make more difficult the establishment of regimes of positive choice. Local authority policies, based on the affirmation of the family, arrange forms of care into a hierarchy of provision, even when this is described as a continuum of care, usually places residential child care at the far end.

Robbins, in a review of English local authorities' child care policies, states that descriptions of residential care as a 'last resort' were few. Most authorities were said to be attempting to "define a new, positive role of residential care, as an effective, time-limited, task-centred resource, offering a range of skills to meet special needs. It should be an 'integrated and flexible' service, a 'rare but positive option' for the 'clearly-identified and defined needs'" (Robbins, 1990).

However, one Social Services Department which specifically ran down use of residential care was Warwickshire (Cliffe, 1990). In 1986, Warwickshire closed the last of its children's homes and the cost savings were channelled into other services for children and families. It did not, however, have a non-residential policy as it had access to places in a voluntary establishment outside the authority and also used residential special schools. At any one time Warwickshire had between one and two percent of children in care placed residentially in care establishments which compares to an average figure nearer to 20 per cent for the English county councils. There was a tight gatekeeping of residential placements which had to be approved by the Director of Social Services. Cliffe comments that many of the young people who ended up in residential care had experienced several failed community placements which could only be damaging for them (Cliffe, 1990).

Warwickshire's achievements was not just in terms of making more use of foster placements but in extending the range of their use; for short-term placements, for new admissions to care, for assessment purposes, and for some adolescents. Cliffe shows that while, generally, assessments of placements achieving their aims was comparable to other research studies, children tended to have a greater number of placements.

Part of the problem in the whole debate about residential child care as a positive choice or as a last resort is the extent to which residential care is perceived as a concrete entity, where the failings of one element transmit to the whole. In fact, we need to create terms to describe which elements of the englobalising term residential child care can be part of a 'positive choice' given the premium set of keeping young people in their families. A main theme of the Wagner Report was that what has previously been described as residential child care should be seen as part of community-based provision. The question is, can all residential child care really become part of such a continuum? Perhaps, establishments which do remove a young person from the community have a legitimate place as a 'last resort'. Not all establishments can become 'family-supplement' oriented, perhaps not all should.

Perhaps we need to think of residential child care in terms of clusters of provision. The first could be termed a cluster of locally-based community provision which would, in residential terms include, crash-pads, short-term respite facilities, local residential resource centres, small children's homes. Importantly, these would link into other forms of community provision, family centres, day-care and Intermediate Treatment. The second cluster would include residential establishments which do not have the same degree or attachment of permeability with the child's home community, where the separation of children is part of the aims of the residential experience. These we have called, for want of a better term, enclosed residential communities. This does not preclude work with the child's family, or with children in their home context. Indeed, research on List D schools and secure accommodation showed that a lack of this type of work had detrimental consequences. This cluster would include secure units, special schools and therapeutic communities.

We have used the term cluster because it does not concretise provision into a hierarchy and because it acknowledges that this distinction operates only along one dimension. Both clusters if viewed along other dimensions would split apart to reflect differing aims and objectives. In the first cluster, we would find a deliberate and definite policy of permeability to the community for any group care (rather than just residential-care) provision. In the second cluster, separation from the child's home community accords with the therapeutic or containment goals of the establishment and is not a secondary factor related to the geographical or social isolation of the residential establishment. Use of group-care in either cluster, at any decision-making point, can be/ought to be a matter of 'positive choice' in terms of the individual child's needs. The selection of the appropriate form of care demands clarity in the aims and objectives of particular residential placements and confidence in its ability to meet needs. The use of residential care as a 'last resort' reflects the lack of both clarity and confidence.

6. APPROPRIATE AND INAPPROPRIATE SANCTIONS AND PUNISHMENTS

Millham et al, in evidence to a DHSS Working Party on discipline and control in residential child-care, state that inappropriate discipline can increase the psychological damage already experienced by children (Millham et al, 1981). They argue that various forms of control are inappropriate. Corporal punishment is ineffective and children and adolescents can be controlled by other means. The threat of transfer or threat of removal to another residential setting is also unacceptable. Research evidence also shows that the transfer of children to secure units is as much to do with the inadequacies of open establishments as it is to do with the behaviour of the children themselves.

While Millham et al suggest that group punishment can be effective in checking a general drift of indiscipline, its use to get an individual to own up to a misdemeanour is not warranted. Limiting access to parents, friends and relatives is an inappropriate sanction and denial of home leave should only be used in situations where serious offences have occurred as a direct result of being on leave. The use of public disapproval is only appropriate as an integrated part of an establishment's philosophy and goals. Similarly Millham et al discouraged the hostile identification of children by forcing them to wear unusual clothes or to eat alone (Millham et al, 1981).

Millham et al make the cogent point that it is easier to point to the adverse effects of established sanctions than to specify effective approaches to the control of disruptive young people. They argue that it is the 'ethos' of the establishment which effectively controls by fashioning a system of mutually held expectations, values and norms of conduct which exercise restraint on members. Young people must perceive that they are getting tangible benefits from the experience of residential care. While there is no prescription for creating a positive 'ethos' in a residential establishment, they suggest five features which seem to be common to all successful establishments: young people should feel enriched by their residential experience; they should see themselves as acquiring clear instrumental skills; the establishment should pursue goals which are matched to the needs which necessitated absence from home rather than those brought about by living away; there should be consensus amongst staff, pupils and parents about what these goals should be along with clear and consistent leadership; and the establishment should make efforts to fragment the informal world of children, for example by creating small group situations (Millham et al, 1981).

Issues of control have obviously been given high profile by the situation of 'pindown' in Staffordshire. At least 132 children were subjected to 'pindown' between November 1983 and October 1989. The Inquiry concluded that the children suffered to varying degrees "the despair and the potentially damaging effects of isolation, the humiliation of having to wear night clothes, knock on the door to 'impart information'" and of having "all their personal possessions removed; and the intense frustration and boredom from the lack of communication, companionship with others and recreation". Pindown was described as "intrinsically unethical, unprofessional and unacceptable" (Staffordshire County Council, 1991).

The 'pindown' experience in Staffordshire shows the degree to which inappropriate sanctions as made explicit by Millham et al (1981) can become routinised, not just in terms of controlling severely disturbed and violent young people, but as a knee-jerk response to any child who is perceived as not conforming to the rules.

The physical and sexual abuse of children within residential establishments can occur in a more informal, secretive way. Unfortunately, this is not uncommon and one of the most recent examples was the abuse of young people in Leicesterhsire children's homes in the early eighties. Concern about the abuse of children in residential care does not simply focus on staff. There is increasing evidence of the problem of the sexual abuse of children by other residents (Fisher and Holloway-Vine, 1990).

7. STRESS, BURNOUT, STAFF TURNOVER AND SUPPORT

Any environment contains stressors and sometimes these stimulate the worker towards better task performance. However, they might also overburden the worker (Cummings and Cooper, 1979; Gardener, 1988; Cranwell-Ward, 1987; Wiener, 1989; Williams 1990). Some authors have indicated that the best way of combating stress is to identify and modify its social and situational sources. To reduce the occurrence of stress to personal difficulties though plausible, is usually misleading (Swanson, 1987).

Mattingly identifies a number of factors which induce stress in residential care situations. Residential institutions are commonly 'closed systems' and workers are relatively isolated both professionally and socially (see Berridge, 1985). There is pressure on staff to present a favourable public image and protect the agency from criticism. Staff, including heads of home, are unable to influence and be meaningfully included in decision-making and they feel that they are not valued. There is a conflict between the worker's commitment, dedication and idealism, essential to caring work, and the frustrations of the reality of the work. The time-limited nature of residential work means staff do not remain involved to see productive growth and resolution of problems. Residential workers may find it difficult to perceive their own effectiveness and this is exacerbated by low levels of training and supervision. There is a tension between the need to empathise with the experience of young people and the need to remain fully adult and not allow young people to be an inappropriate participant in their own psychological conflicts. Finally, there is a lack of privacy for those residential workers who 'live in' (Mattingly, 1981).

An important stressor, not touched upon by Mattingly, is the sexual behaviour of residents. Fear of the possible consequences, such as vulnerability to allegations by children may well be the biggest barrier to close relationships between staff and adolescents (Beddoe et al, 1980; see also White, 1987). But the sense of sexual morals, sexual maturity and sexuality of workers in relation to other workers and to the young men and young women in their care is also a source of stress and tension (White, 1987).

Failure to provide clarity in relation to the functions and objectives of residential child care can also be a source of stress. Unclear management policies, uncertain lines of command and poor communication with colleagues can reinforce this stress (Boddoe, 1980; see Utting, 1991).

The term 'burnout' is used to describe a condition found in a variety of situations which involve work with people as their 'carers' or 'teachers'. Pines et al (1981) suggest that burnout is physical, emotional or attitudinal exhaustion related to occupational stress. Maslach and Jackson (1981), state that 'burnout' has 3 main characteristics: visible aspects such as increased feelings of emotional exhaustion; negative cynical depersonalisation; and evaluations of oneself which are negative and lack a feeling of personal accomplishment (Maslach and Jackson, 1981, cited in Swanson, 1987, p. 11).

Mattingly argues that 'burnout' is part of a process, either for the group or individual. It begins as a vague feeling of discontent and the worker begins to doubt his/her caring work. Feelings of inadequacy link to an uncomfortable rigidity in thinking and behaviour. At this point, although a worker may feel inadequate, it may not have any obvious objective effect on their work. However, at some point, feelings of inadequacy, emotional or physical exhaustion and low morale, will surface, even if only intermittently. The 'burning-out' worker becomes more apparent. However, this may only lead to a more sophisticated level of denial on the part of co-workers, which in turn creates an additional stressor in the burn-out process (Mattingly, 1981).

This denial of support adds a further twist to the process of burn-out. The worker may then experience a sense of drift between interpretations of 'reality' as he and his colleagues understand it. A worker undermined in this way, dissatisfied with his/her performance, may begin to work even harder, work longer hours, make great sacrifices over his/her personal time and space. These actions, if initiated by a lack of energy and/or feelings of professional/personal inadequacy, will tend to increase stress and further deplete the worker's level of emotional energy. The downward spiral, is thus continued and given added momentum. The differences in perceptions between the burning-out worker and other staff members may lead to loss of trust. At some point the problem of the 'burning-out' individual has to be dealt with. Often this might mean the person leaves, either of their own accord (but in accordance with group pressure) or they are 'counselled' out of their job. This relieves the immediate problem. However, if the person does not leave or, if the stresses are great enough, the symptoms of burnout will extend to other staff and it is not unusual for several members of a work group to burnout simultaneously. Beset by ongoing stressors and by the cumulative stress encountered in the burnout process, either on an individual or group base, the physical health of workers begins to deteriorate (Mattingly, 1981).

Burnout can be seen as a condition in which it is too late to take 'constructive action' and the result can be increased staff turnover (Beddoe, 1980). There are many reasons for staff turnover, not just stress and burnout, for example, staff promotion or staff may leave for training. Berridge, in his earlier study of staff turnover argued that there were 2 main reasons for staff turnover: the peculiar demands of residential child care: and the 'turnover-prone' nature of staff recruited into this sector (Berridge, 1981). Berridge suggests that it also is important to look at biographical factors as important 'external' reasons for turnover. He surveyed the employment characteristics of residential child care staff in England in the 1970s and concluded that typically these workers were young, female and had little training. Therefore a high turnover rate would be expected.

Berridge questioned ex-residential workers about their reasons for leaving. He found that the experience of stress is an important factor in explaining the high level of staff turnover in community homes. One in 5 said that emotional and physical pressures were at least partly responsible for the decision to leave. Almost two-thirds of respondents reported that the work was different from what they had expected. A large majority said that they had received inadequate support in their work (Berridge, 1981).

In their discussion of how to cope with stress, the RCA Working Party divide the phenomenon of stress into two. On the one hand, there is stress which is inevitable and this must be alleviated; on the other, there is stress which is avoidable and this must be eliminated (Beddoe, 1980). It is the task of workers and management to support each other to alleviate 'necessary' stressors and eliminate 'unnecessary' stressors.

Support has at least 2 dimensions; general support which involves provision of adequate resources to the residential establishment; and an interpersonal response, at the level of relations between individuals and in group contexts such as team meetings. The first task is to identify stress factors. Problems need to be shared and this may involve someone outwith line-management such as a consultant, friends and family or trade union and professional association representatives (Beddoe, 1980).

Mattingly also discusses the ways in which stress can be tackled. The basis for support rests on the ability of the worker to articulate their awareness of stress and as an initial stage in this residential workers need to seriously reflect on the reasons they are doing the work and the rewards they gain from it. They also need to be able to identify areas of personal skills and competence. The structure of the worker's personal life is also very important in the management of stress: patterns of eating and drinking, of sleep and recreation. The development of competencies will reduce stress further (Mattingly, 1981).

All of these activities can be supported by management and if this occurs the level of support is magnified and staff will feel valued. This in turn will further increase resistance to stressors. Effective management will focus on a flexible approach to shift-systems, including use of 'time-outs' for staff who have faced especially stressful circumstances. Importantly, managements should use supervision regularly and effectively, by making sure that strengths as well as weaknesses are recognised.

8. TRAINING OF RESIDENTIAL CHILD CARE STAFF

The low levels of qualification and training among residential staff is not a new issue. Barr (1987) outlines the history of training in this field and what becomes clear is that training has never had a high priority and where it has been seen as important, it has often fallen into abeyance (Ainsworth, 1981). Each public service has had a separate history in the field of residential qualification. Even after the impact of the second world war and the Curtis and Clyde Reports, new local authority residential provision was segregated from other provision for children in need. Training, validated by a Central Training Council in Child Care (CTC), was likewise separated and specialist. 'Housemother courses' began in 1947/48 under the title of 'Certificate in the Residential Care of Children' (CRCC), followed in 1957 by the 'Certificate in the Residential Care of Children and Young People' (CRCCYP). Additionally, in 1959, an 'Advanced Certificate in the Residential Care of Children and Young People' (ACRCCYP), (later retitled Senior Certificate) was created (Barr, 1987).

In Scotland, there were parallel developments, the Scottish Advisory Council in Child Care awarded a CRCC taught over a year. More experienced staff could attend a one-year course to obtain a Senior Certificate in Residential Child Care (SCRCC). Barr describes the content of these courses as fairly domestic and practical. The CRCCYP was created to meet changing demands and courses expanded to cover more detailed study of very young children and of adolescents. The SCRCCYP began to address questions related to supervision and management of residential staff. Despite this variety of courses, residential staff in the 1960s were still largely untrained and unqualified (Working Party Z, 1969).

Towards the end of the 1960s, the idea of 'generic social work', was taking root. The general push towards this concept, which combined social work services to different client groups within the same organisation and occupational role, involved a rethink of the role of residential work. Necessarily it also involved a rethink of training. The Castle Priory conference in 1968 came out strongly in favour of joint training for residential and field workers.

The Central Council for Education and Training in Social Work (CCETSW) replaced the CTC in 1971. The members-designate of CCETSW agreed with the Castle Priory Report. Their view was that there ought not to be separate certificates in residential work. Nevertheless there were considerable problems to overcome in implementing this view. For example the very large number of residential staff and the range of their training needs within a two-year timescale. Given these problems, a new qualification, the Certificate in Social Service (CSS) emerged in the 1970s. It was intended to offer a qualification to residential staff. However, from the beginning it was criticised as being divisive as it tended to give a lower status qualification as compared to the CQSW, despite rhetoric to the contrary (Barr, 1987).

The CQSW was considered as a qualification for social work in residential care. However, CQSW courses during the 1970s and 1980s were criticised as not offering enough to students wishing to do residential work with young people and not giving enough consideration to the specialist needs of residential workers. The RCA report on training in residential care called for more opportunities for post-qualifying specialist training aimed at meeting the needs of residential and day-care staff.

In the period of transition between CRCCYP one-year full-time courses and CQSW/CSS courses, Millham et al (1980) conducted research on the backgrounds of residential social work students and their training course experience. They found that students on the CRCCYP courses tended to be younger, had left school by the age of 16 and to have had numerous jobs after leaving school. The authors concluded that the differing backgrounds of the 2 groups of students would encourage fragmentation and conflict on generic courses (Millham et al, 1980). Over all the courses, only slightly more than half of the students considered that college-based courses were the best way of improving social work practice.

The vast majority of students who responded to the follow-up survey experienced difficulties on return to work. Students found difficulty in re-establishing their roles in the work situation. Importantly, students were more aware in their practice of the importance of the families of children, field social workers and the local community. They were more committed to involving them in their residential work (Millham et al, 1980).

In discussing the need for specialist residential training, Millham et al comment that generic child care training tends to obscure the differences between fieldwork and residential work. They stress the importance of in-house training for residential staff; for induction courses for new staff and more short courses for incumbent staff (Millham et al, 1980). They also stress the need to make training opportunities as flexible as possible.

The new Diploma in Social Work replaces both the CQSW and the CSS. Currently similar problems and issues constitute part of the debate concerning how and if training for residential work can be incorporated into Diploma programs.

9. UNIT SIZE, SHIFT SYSTEMS AND STAFFING LEVELS

An optimum unit size does not exist in the abstract. The aims and functions of homes have to be considered. Moreover, unit size must also relate in some way to shift systems and staffing levels. A shift system organises the delivery of the main resource available to the children, the staff. Therefore, shift systems can influence perceptions of the optimum size of unit as well as the optimum staffing level. It follows from this that the nature of the optimum shift system and staffing level is also tied to the aims of the home. The clearer these aims are, the more we are able to say whether the unit size is too great, or whether the shift system is inappropriate and whether the staffing level is inadequate.

Unit size is historically connected to the rhetoric surrounding the 'mouldering bastions' which local authorities inherited from the Poor Law (Packman, 1981). The Curtis Committee made recommendations about unit size, linked to the intended role of the children's home and favoured small group homes containing not more than 12 children of various ages. There was a clear attempt to simulate ordinary family life (Packman, 1981).

The Curtis Committee had been concerned with child care and deprivation. However, by the early 1960s and certainly by the early 1970s, the connection between deprivation and delinquency had been clearly drawn. In the context of Seebohm and Kilbrandon, services to these groups were no longer being seen as separate. Moreover, increasingly social workers and others were saying that children in residential care were more emotionally or behaviourally disturbed. In this context, the appropriateness of the family group home as a resource which could deal with the origins or treatment of delinquency was questioned. But the unit size of these homes was implicitly connected to their supposed role - to be 'like a family'.

If the role of residential care was something different than the group home, a different unit size might be thought appropriate. In some respects, this was a fait accompli. In England and Wales, as a result of Children and Young Persons Act 1969, Approved Schools became the responsibility of local authorities. They became known as Community Homes with Education (CHEs). Generally speaking these CHEs were large with an average of 89 places per school (Gill, 1974). Moreover, until the mid 1980s the pressure to use residential child care was constant despite continuing rhetoric against institutional solutions. This pressure tended to maintain existing levels of occupancy and unit size.

The situation has since changed. The pressure to reduce the numbers of children in local authority children's homes has increased in line with the pressure for 'community care' (Stainton-Rogers, 1988). There is also the development of residential staff engaging in more extensive and flexible work with the family and community. There are indications that this thinking is developing in the field. Small is again beautiful, whether or not the child or young person is seen to require temporary or long-term care, nurturing or independence training.

In relation to shift systems, we have found no specific work on this issue. This, in itself, is quite strange, given that staff are the primary resource in any residential establishment and the shift system is fundamentally important in determining how a service can be delivered (King et al, 1971). What can easily be noted is the shift from the family group home, with its 'resident matriarchal figures', to whom a shift system is almost 'anathema' (Berridge, 1985), to the 'multi-purpose' home in which staff are not resident and a shift system is crucial.

Fulcher and Ainsworth (1981) discuss 11 different variables necessary for comparative study of residential establishments and 2 of these relate to shift systems; 'personal complement and deployment' and 'patterns in the use of time and activity'. Staff rotas or schedules, they state, often become a focus of discussion of children and staff as they try to find out who should be doing what (Fulcher and Ainsworth, 1981). The shift-system structures staff-time and determines who can speak to who and at what time.

Fraser (1989) compared the shift system in one children's home with the shift-system which the Harlesden Community Project had in the 1970s. This was because Harlesden had conducted significant work outwith the residential unit. Harlesden had a similar staffing ratio, but managed to allocate 40 per cent of total staff-time in the shift-system to external work. In the home studied by Fraser, external work was not specifically allocated by the shift-system. Fraser found that the shift-system generally did not allow workers to conduct extensive duties outside the home without recourse to overtime payments or time-in-lieu.

In relation to staffing levels in residential care, 2 publications are of note. The Castle Priory conference report, 'The Residential Task in Child Care' and 'Staffing Ratios in Residential Establishments: A Platform for the 1980's Lane implies that this work has already been done by the Castle Priory report. Lane states that there are many ways of calculating staffing requirements, and the problem facing any person devising a formula is the conflict between the need to keep calculations simple and the need to take account of the large number of important variables (Lane, 1980).

The paucity of written work on staffing levels may have something to do with a point made in the Wagner Report. In commenting on the fact that the Castle Priory Report is dated, it points out that the "sheer variety of residential services renders meaningless any simple method of calculating staffing requirements ...." (Wagner, 1988). However, explicitly or implicitly, this does not stop various authors from arguing that many residential child care establishments are understaffed. The Castle Priory Report, though dated, can still be useful in this respect.

10. THE ECONOMIC COSTS OF RESIDENTIAL CHILD CARE

The cost of residential child care has been shown to be influenced by a variety of factors: labour costs; occupancy and turnover rates; specialisation of homes; and the quality of care in terms of the physical environment. Economies of scale operate which minimise operating costs (excluding capital costs and non-residential costs) at approximately 12 places (Knapp and Smith, 1985). The characteristics of the children being cared for were also important. The age of the children; the proportion of female residents and the proportion of "mentally handicapped" residents were significant in cost terms. Knapp and Smith acknowledge, however, that their data did not include indicators of some of the principal dimensions of difficulty in relation to the behaviour of the children.

The provision of non-residential services such as preventive and emergency day-care, day care for home-on-trial support, or after care support increased costs, as did the provision of social care tasks outside the home with both residents and non-residents.

Knapp and Smith argue that many of the variables entering the cost function could be beyond the control of authorities in the medium and short-term and they argue the Audit Commission's assumption that cost differences between authorities reflect differences in efficiency is flawed.

The cost argument has provided a deal of support for the shift in emphasis between residential care and fostering and Parker commented that there was the happy coincidence that the most desirable provision was for once the most economical (Parker, 1966). It has been argued, however, that the costing of foster care rarely takes into account the hidden costs of social work support, advertising, administration and research (Walton and Elliot, 1980; Knapp and Robertson, 1988).

Of course hidden costs are not solely confined to fostering. Residential care itself will have hidden costs over and above those of direct service provision. In a survey conducted in 1983 in Mid-Glamorgan Social Services Department, this non-residential cost element was equivalent to an average of 8.7 per cent of the total cost. The largest component of this was accounted for by field social worker time (Knapp and Baines, 1987).

Another factor which affects the comparison of costs between fostering and residential care is the degree to which like is compared with like in terms of the children themselves. Davies and Knapp (1988) argue that the average cost of care will be positively associated with the difficulties displayed by children. As a larger proportion of children are fostered, then the average difficulty of these children will increase and this will increase the average cost of foster care. However, the average difficulty of children in residential care will also increase, thus increasing the average cost of residential care. Knapp argues that while recommendations to increase the use of foster care are not inappropriate, the commonly expressed cost argument seriously under-estimates the future costs of foster care and dangerously exaggerates the savings that will flow from changes in the balance of care (Knapp, 1988).

11. RESEARCH NEEDS

Little research had been done in Scotland in relation to what we have termed the cluster of community-based residential establishments. Most of the Scottish research has been conducted on List D schools and on secure accommodation linked to them although this is now becoming dated. While in England, a number of studies, notably Berridge (1985) and Knapp and Smith (1984), shed light on community children's homes, the same has not occurred in Scotland. There is an urgent need for detailed research on the experience of residential child care. This research, we believe, needs to focus on a number of issues.

Firstly, there needs to be a survey of existing residential provision. The survey could focus on the nature of residential provision; the extent to which residential establishments provide non-residential services; the number and qualifications of residential staff; and the characteristics of the resident population.

The assessment of children for residential placements and the decision-making process which places children in residential establishments also requires study. The manner in which the needs of children are assessed and the way in which such assessments are used in the various decision-making structures of Social Work Departments, Education Departments and Children's Hearings are of crucial importance to the matching of children to placements as a positive choice.

For such decision-making to be rational, there needs to be information on what actually happens in residential establishments. What are the aims and objectives of individual units and to what degree are they able to achieve those objectives. There are different elements of this issue which need further research.

Work needs to be done across the range of residential provision (children's homes, resource centres, family centres, special schools) to identify the degree to which there are coherent and explicit statements and programmes of intervention with the resident children. The actual work of these establishments then needs to be studied in detail to discover the extent to which practice follows these programmes.

The impact of residential intervention must obviously be related to the outcomes for the children and young people resident in the establishments. We see the need for 2 types of outcome study. The first would be a short to medium term outcome study of the effect of residential placements and the intervention programmes being used in various establishments. This would focus on the outcomes of children and young people until they leave the residential placement. The second type of outcome study would cover a much longer period and would follow young people through the placement and onto independence and early adulthood. Such a study would be problematic in terms of attempting to keep track of young people once they had left care, but it is important that the outcomes of social work intervention are seen in the wider context of young people's lives rather than just the immediate situation of their being in care. An important aspect of such research are consumer surveys which look at the experiences, outlook and perceptions of young people in residential care.

The use of secure accommodation, including the use of secure rooms in residential establishments, also deserves further study. This would need to be investigated in the wider context of the control of violent and aggressive young people in all types of residential establishment.

Finally, the links of residential establishments to both their own local community and to the community of the child's own family need further investigation. There is a rhetoric concerning community care which needs to be critically unpacked through empirical research.

Research is only of use if there is a political will to respond to its findings. Many of the issues described in this paper are not new. For example, the pay, status and training of residential workers has been on the agenda for many years. In 1975, Newman and Mackintosh commented that residential workers doubted whether their report and recommendations would change things. Their doubts seem justified.

Bibliography

Ackland, J W, (1982) *Girls in Care: A Case Study of Residential Treatment*, Gower, Aldershot.

Ainsworth, F, (1980) The Training of Group Care Personnel in the Personal Social Services, in Walton, R G and Elliot, D (eds) *Residential Care: A reader in Current Theory and Practice*, Pergamon Press, Oxford.

Ainsworth, F, (1981) The Training of Personnel for *Group Care with Children, in Ainsworth, F and Fulcher, L (eds) Group Care for Children, Concept and Issues*, Tavistock, London.

Ainsworth, F and Fulcher, L C, (eds), (1981) *Group Care for Children: Concept and Issues*, Tavistock, London.

Ainsworth, F and Walker, M, (1983) A *Practice Curriculum for Group Care*, Paper 14.2, CCETSW, London.

Aldgate, J, (1977), *The Identification of Factors influencing Children's Length of Stay in Care*, PhD thesis (unpublished), University of Edinburgh.

Aldgate, J, (1980) Identification of factors influencing children's length of stay in care, in Triseliotis (ed) *New Developments in Foster Care and Adoption*, RKP, London.

Aldgate, J, Pratt, R and Duggan, M, (1989) Using Care Away from Home to Prevent Family Breakdown, *Adoption and Fostering*, vol 13, pp 32-27.

Baker, R, (1986) The Experience of Burnout among Social Workers: Towards an Understanding of Behavioural Reactions, in Marshall, M Preston-Shoot, M and Wincott, E (eds), *Skills for Social Workers in the 80's*, BASW, Birmingham.

Balbernie, R, (1973) The Cotswold Experiment, *Community Schools Gazette*, vol 66 No 10, pp 532-565.

Baldwin, N, (1990) *The Power to Care in Children's Homes: Experiences of residential workers*, Gower, Aldershot.

Barclay Committee, (1982), *Social Workers: Their Roles and Tasks*, National Institute for Social Work, Bedford Square Press, London.

Barker, P, (1988) The Future of Residential Treatment for Children, in Schaefer, C E and Swanson A J (eds) *Children in Residential Care: Critical Issues in Treatment*, Van Nostrand Reinhold, New York.

Barlow, G, (1979) The Youth Treatment Centre, in Payne, C J and White, K J (eds), *Caring for Deprived Children: International Case Studies of Residential Settings*, RCA, Croom Helm, London.

Barr, H, (1987) *Perspectives on Training for Residential Work*, CCETSW, London.

Beedell, C, (1970) *Residential Life with Children*, RKP, London.

Beddoe, C, (1980) *Stress in Residential Work*, A Report to the RCA AGM 1980 by a Working Party, Residential Care Association.

Beker, J, (1981) New Roles for Group Care Centres, in Ainsworth, F and Fulcher, L (eds) Group Care for Children: Concept and Issues, Tavistock, London.

Belknap, I, (1956) *Human Problems of a State Mental Hospital*, Springer, New York.

Beresford, P and Croft, S, (1984) Living Together: A Redefinition of Group Care Services, in Philpot T (ed) *Group Care Practice: the Challenge of the Next Decade*, Community Care, Business Press International, Sutton.

Beresford, P, Kemmis, J and Tunstil, J, (1987) *In Care in North Battersea*, North Battersea Research Group, London.

Berridge, D, (1981) *Other People's Children: A Study of Staff Turnover in Community Homes*, PhD Thesis, University of Bristol.

Berridge, D, (1985) *Children's Homes*, Basil Blackwell, Oxford.

Bilson, A and Thorpe, D, (1987) *Child Care Careers and Their Management: A Systems Perspective*, Fife Regional Council Social Work Department, Glenrothes.

Black, A, (1988) Residential and Community Care - The Local Authorities' View, in Wilkinson, J E and O'Hara, G (eds), *Our Children: Residential and Community Care*, National Children's Bureau (Scottish Group), London.

Bowlby, J, (1953) *Child Care and the Growth of Love*, Pelican.

Brown, B J and Christie, M, (1981) *Social Learning Practice in Residential Child Care*, Pergamon, Oxford.

Brown, G, Bone, M, Dalison, and Wing, J K, (1966) *Schizophrenia and Social Care*, Oxford University Press.

Bruce, N and Spencer, J C, (1976) *Face to Face with Families: A Report on the Children's Panels in Scotland*, Macdonald, Loanhead.

Bruce, N, (1982) Historical Background, in Martin, F and Murray, K (eds), *The Scottish Juvenile Justice System*, Scottish Academic Press, Edinburgh.

Bullock, R, Hosie, K, Little, M and Millham, S, (1990) Secure Accommodation for Very Difficult Adolescents: Some Recent Research Findings, *Journal of Adolescence*, vol 13, pp 205-216.

Castle Priory Conference Report, (1969) *The Residential Task in Child Care*, RCA.

Caudill, W, (1958) *The Psychiatric Hospital as a Small Society*, Harvard University Press, Cambridge MA.

Cawson, P and Martell, M, (1979) *Children Referred to Closed Units*, HMSO, London.

Cherniss, C, (1980) *Professional Burnout in Human Service Organisations*, Praeger, New York, 1980.

Children's Panel Chairmen's Group, (1989) *Study of Children's Hearings' Disposals in Relation to Resources*, Children's Panel Chairmen's Group.

Cliffe, D, (1990) *An End to Residential Child Care? The Warwickshire Direction*, conference paper, National Children's Bureau/Warwickshire County Council.

Community Homes Schools Gazette, (1978) *Training Needs and Resources: a Report to the Association of Community Homes Schools*, August 1978.

Cornish, D B and Clarke, R V G, (1975) *Residential Treatment and its Effects upon Delinquency*, Home Office Research Studies, HMSO, London.

Cowperthwaite, D J, (1988) *The Emergence of the Scottish Children's Hearings System: An Administrative/Political Study of the Establishment of Novel Arrangements in Scotland for Dealing with Juvenile Offenders - 1960-1982,* Institute of Criminal Justice, Faculty of Law, University of Southampton.

Cox, D and McArdle, I, (1986) *The Druid's Heath Experience: Progressive child care in action,* Birmingham Polytechnic/Barnardo's.

Cranwell-Ward, J, (1987) *Managing Stress,* Gower, Aldershot.

Cummings, T, and Cooper, C (1979) A Cybernetic Framework for Studying Occupational Stress, *Human Relations,* vol 32 No 5, pp 395-418.

Davies, B and Knapp, M, (1988) Costs and Residential Social Care, in I Sinclair (ed) *Residential Care, The Research Reviewed,* National Institute for Social Work, HMSO, London.

Davis, A, (1981) *The Residential Solution: State Alternatives to Family Care,* Tavistock, London.

Davis, L, (1982) *Residential Care: A Community Resource,* Heinemann, London.

Denham, E, (1984) *The Use of Unruly Certificates,* Scottish Office, Edinburgh.

Deutsch, A, (1973) *The Shame of the States,* Arno, New York.

Dharamsi, F Edmonds, G Filkin, E Headley, C Jones, P Naish, M Scott, I Smith, E Smith, H Williams, J, (1979) *Community Work and Caring for Children: A community project in an inner city local authority by a group of workers from the Harlesden Community Project, 1971-1976,* Owen Wells, Ilkley.

DHSS, (1981) *Control and Discipline in Community Homes: a Report of Working Party.*

DHSS, (1986a) *Children in Care in England and Wales,* HMSO, London.

DHSS, (1986b) *Inspection of Community Homes, 1985,* DHSS Social Services Inspectorate.

DHSS, (1987) *The Law on Child Care and Family Services,* HMSO, London.

Douglas, T (ed), (1980) *Admission to Residential Care,* Tavistock, London.

Dydyk, B J, French, G, Gertsman, C, Morrison, N and O'Neill, I, (1989) Admitting Whole Families: An Alternative to Residential Care, *Canadian Journal of Psychiatry,* vol 34, Oct 1989, pp 694-698.

Dunham, J, (1978) Staff Stress in Residential Work, *Social Work Today,* 19(45), pp 18-20.

Dunham, H and Weinberg, K, (1960) *The Culture of a State Mental Hospital,* Wayne State University Press, Detroit.

Edwards, P and Miltenberger, R (1991) Burnout Among Staff Members at Community Residential Facilities for Persons with Mental Retardation, *Mental Retardation,* vol 29, No 3, pp 125-128.

Equality for Children, (1983) *Keeping Kids out of Care,* Equality For Children Group, London.

Fisher, D and Holloway-Vine, J, (1990), *Nottinghamshire Young Sex Offenders Group,* information paper.

Ford, R, (1982) Consequences, in Martin, F and Murray, K (eds), *The Scottish Juvenile Justice System,* Scottish Academic Press, Edinburgh.

Fraser, A W, (1989) *The Evaluation of Fraserburgh Children's Home with New Child Care Policies: An Illuminative Evaluation*, PhD Thesis (unpublished), University of Aberdeen.

Fratter, J, Newton, D and Shinegold, D, (1982) *Cambridge Cottage Pre-Fostering and Adoption Unit*, Barnardo Social Work Papers 16, Dr Barnardo's, Barkingside.

Freudenberger, H J (1975) The Staff Burnout Syndrome in Alternative Institutions, *Psychotherapy: Theory, Research and Practice*, vol 12 No 1, pp 73-82.

Freudenberger, H (1977) Burn-Out: Occupational Hazard of the Child Care Worker, *Child Care Quarterly*, vol 6, No 2.

Frost, N and Stein, M, (1989) *The Politics of Child Welfare: Inequality, Power and Change*, Harvester Wheatsheaf, London.

Fulcher, L and Ainsworth, F, (1981) Planned Care and Treatment: The Notion of Programme, in Ainsworth, F and Fulcher, L (eds) *Group Care for Children: Concept and Issues*, Tavistock, London.

Gardener, D, (1988) A Sharing Approach to the Management of Stress, *Social Work Today*, pp 6-18.

Gill, O, (1974) *Whitegate: An Approved School in Transition*, Liverpool University Press.

Goffman, E, (1968) *Asylums, Essays of the Social Situation of Mental Patients and Other Inmates*, Penguin, Harmondsworth.

Hansen, P, (1988) *Tasks of Residential Workers: A Study of Direct Care Practitioners*, Avebury, Aldershot.

Harris, H and Lipman, A, (1984) Gender and the Pursuit of Respectability: Dilemmas of Daily Life in a Home for Adolescents, *British Journal of Social Work*, vol 14, pp 265-275.

Hazel, N, (1981) *A Bridge to Independence*, Basil Blackwell, Oxford.

Hewitt, L H, (1979) *Work Characteristics, Quality of Supervision and Job Stress in Child Care*, Unpublished Master's thesis, University of Pittsburgh.

Hey, A, (1973) Analysis and Definition of the Functions of Caring Establishments, in Hunter, J and Ainsworth F (eds) *Residential Establishments: The Evolving of Caring Systems*, School of Social Administration, University of Dundee.

Heywood, J, (1965) *Children in care: The development of the service for the deprived child*, RKP, London.

Holman, R, (1980) *Inequality in Child Care*, Child Poverty Action Group, London.

Holtom, C, (1972) *Staff Stress in Working with Disturbed Adolescents*, Proceedings of the Seventh Conference of the Association for the Psychiatric Study of Adolescents.

Hyman, R, (1970) Economic motivation and labour stability, British *Journal of Industrial Relations*, vol 8, pp 159-178

Jones, H, (1979) *The Residential Community: A setting for social work*, RKP, London.

Kahan, B, (1979) *Growing Up in Care: Ten People Talking*, Basil Blackwell, Oxford.

Kearney, B, (1987) *Children's Hearings and the Sheriff Court*, Butterworths, London.

Kelly, B and Littlewood, P (1983) *Factors Underlying the Referrals and Commitals Processes Relating to a Secure Unit for Young People (I)*, Report to the Social Work Services Group, Sociology Department, University of Glasgow.

Kelly, B and Littlewood, P (1985a) *Factors Underlying the Referrals and Commitals Processes Relating to a Secure Unit for Young People (II)*, Report to the Social Work Services Group, Sociology Department, University of Glasgow.

Kelly, B and Littlewood, P (1985b) *A Sociological Study of Life in a Secure Unit for Children and Young People,* Report to the Social Work Services Group, Sociology Department, University of Glasgow.

Kelsall, J and McCullough, B, (1988) *Family Work in Residential Child Care: Partnership in Practice,* Boys' and Girls' Welfare Society, Manchester Free Press, Cheadle.

Kilbrandon Report, (1964) *Children and Young Persons, Scotland,* HMSO, Edinburgh.

King, M, (1988) The Role and Content of Residential Care, in J E Wilkinson and G O'Hara (eds) *Our Children: Residential and Community Care,* National Children's Bureau, London.

King, R D, Raynes, N V and Tizard, J, (1971) *Patterns of Residential Care: Sociological Studies in Institutions for Handicapped Children,* RKP, London.

Knapp, M, (1986) The Field Social Work Implications of Residential Child Care, *British Journal of Social Work,* vol 16, pp 25-48.

Knapp, M and Baines, B (1987) Hidden Cost Multipliers for Residential Child Care, *Local Government Studies,* vol 13, No 4, pp 53-73.

Knapp, M and Smith, J, (1984) *The PSSRU National Survey of Children's Homes,* Report No 2, discussion paper 322, Personal Social Services Research Unit, University of Kent.

Knapp, M and Smith, J (1985) The Costs of Residential Child Care: Explaining Variations in the Public Sector, *Policy and Politics,* vol 13, No 2, pp 127-154.

Knapp, M, Baines, B and Gerrard, B, (1990) Performance Measurement in Child Care: When a Falling Boarding Out Rate should Attract Congratulation and not Castigation, *Policy and Politics,* vol 18, No 1, pp 39-42.

Knapp, M and Robertson, E, (1988) The Cost of Services, in Kahan, B (ed), *Child Care Research, Policy and Practice,* Hodder & Stoughton, London.

Lambert, R, (1964) in Kalton, G, *The Public Schools: A Factual Study of Headmasters' Conference schools in England and Wales,* Longmans.

Lambert, R, Millham, S and Bullock, R, (1969) *Boarding School Education: A Sociology Study,* Weidenfield and Nicolson, London.

Lambert, R, Hipkin, J and Stagg, S, (1968) *New Wine in Old Bottles: Studies in Integration with the Public Schools,* Bell and Co, London.

Lambert, R, Bullock, R and Millham, S, (1970) *A Manual to the Sociology of the School,* Weidenfield and Nicolson, London.

Lambert, R, Bullock, R Millham, S, (1975) *The Chance of a Lifetime,* Weidenfield and Nicolson, London.

Lane, D and Poad, V, (1980) *A Platform for the 1980's: Staffing Ratios in Residential Establishments,* RCA.

Laxton, M (1986) Coordinated Care - A Model for the 80s, *Scottish Child*, No 12, pp 1-3.

Lee, P and Pithers, D, (1980) Radical residential care: Trojan Horse or Non-Runner, in Brake, M and Bailey, R (eds), *Radical Social Work and Practice*, Edward Arnold, London.

Lennox, D, (1982) *Residential Group Therapy for Children*, Tavistock, London.

Littlewood, P, (1987) *Care Appropriate to their Needs? Summary of a Sociological Study of a Secure Unit for Children in Scotland (1982-1986)*, Central Research Unit Papers, Scottish Office, Edinburgh.

Littlewood, P and Kelly B, (1986) *After Release: A Report on The Processes Surrounding the Release of Young People from the Ogilvie Wing Secure Unit, and their Perception of these Processes*, Report to the Social Work Services Group, Sociology Department, University of Glasgow.

Malek, M (1991) *Psychiatric Admissions*, The Children's Society, London.

Manning, N, (1987) What is a Social Problem, in Loney, M *The State or the Market: Politics and Welfare in Contemporary Britain*, Sage Publications, London.

Mapstone, E, (1983) *Crossing the Boundaries: New Directions in the Mental Health Services for Children and Young People in Scotland*, HMSO, Edinburgh.

March, J and Simon, H (1958) *Organisations*, Wiley, London.

Marks, R B, (1973) Institutions for Dependent and Delinquent Children: Histories, Nineteenth-Century Statistics, and Recurrent Goals, in Pappenfort, D M Kilpatrick, D M and Roberts, R W (eds), *Child Caring: Social Policy and the Institution*, Aldine, Chicago.

Martin, F M, Fox, S J and Murray, K, (1981) *Children Out of Court*, Scottish Academic Press, Edinburgh.

Maslach, C, (1982) *Burnout: The Cost of Caring*, Prentice Hall, New Jersey.

Maslach, C and Jackson, S E, (1981) *Maslach Burnout Inventory*, Consulting Lists Press, California.

Maslach, C and Pines, A (1977) The Burn-Out Syndrome in the Day Care Setting, *Child Care Quarterly*, vol 6, No 2, pp 100-113.

Mattingly, M A (1981) Occupational Stress for Group Care Personnel, in Ainsworth, F and Fulcher, L C (eds) *Group Care for Children: Concept and Issues*, Tavistock, London.

Mayer, M F Richman, L H and Balcerzak, E A, (1978) *Group Care of Children: Crossroads and Transitions*, Child Welfare League of America, New York.

McLean, S A M and Docherty, C J, (1984) *The Prosecution of Children in Scotland*, Scottish Office, Edinburgh.

Miller, E and Gwynne, G, (1972) A *Life Apart*, Tavistock, London.

Millham, S, Bullock, R and Hosie, K, (1978) *Locking Up Children: Secure provision within the child-care system*, Saxon House, Farnborough.

Millham, S, Bullock, R, and Hosie, K, (1980) *Learning to Care: The Training of Staff for Residential Social Work with Young People*, Gower, Farnborough.

Millham, S, Bullock, R Hosie, K and Haak, M, (1981) *Issues of Control in Residential Child-care*, HMSO, London.

Millham, S, Bullock R Cherret, P, (1975) *After Grace: Teeth! A Comparative Study of the Residential Experience of Boys in Approved Schools*, Human Context Books.

Millham, S, Bullock R, Hosie, K and Haak, M, (1986) *Lost in Care: The Problems of Maintaining Links between Children in Care and their Families*, Gower, Aldershot.

Monsky, S, (1963) *Staffing of Local Authority Residential Homes for Children*, SS 335, Central Office of Information, London.

Morgan-Klein, B, (1985) *Where am I going to stay: A report on young people leaving care in Scotland*, Scottish Council for Single Homeless, Edinburgh.

Morris, A and McIsaac, M, (1978) *Juvenile Justice? The Practice of Social Welfare*, Heinemann, London.

Moss, P, (1975) Residential care of children: a general view, in Tizard et al, *Varieties of Residential Experience*, RKP, London.

NES (North-East of Scotland Joint Consultative Committee on Residential Child Care Services), (1973) *The Distribution and Use of Residential Child Care Facilities in North-East Scotland*, Aberdeen Peoples Press, Aberdeen.

Newman, N and Mackintosh, H, (1975) *A Roof Over their Heads? Residential Provision for Children in South East Scotland*, University of Edinburgh Department of Social Administration, Edinburgh.

Packman, J, (1981) *The Child's Generation: Child Care Policy in Britain*, Basil Blackwell, Oxford.

Packman, J, Randall, J and Jacques, N (1986) *Who Needs Care? Social Work Decisions about Children*, Basil Blackwell, Oxford.

Page, R and Clarke, G A (eds), (1977) *Who Cares? Young People in Care Speak Out*, National Children's Bureau, London.

Parker, R A, (1988a) An Historical Background to Residential Care, in *Residential Care: The Research Reviewed*, London, National Institute for Social Work, HMSO, London.

Parker, R A (1988b) Residential Care for Children, in I Sinclair (ed) *Residential Care: The Research Reviewed*, National Institute for Social Work, HMSO, London.

Parker, R A, (1966) *Decisions in Child Care*, George Allen and Unwin, London.

Parkin, W, (1989) Private Experiences in the Public Domain: Sexuality and Residential Care Organizations, in Hearn, J (ed), *The Sexuality of Organizations*, Sage Publications, London.

Payne, C J, (1977) Residential Social Work, in Sprecht, H and Vickery, A (eds), *Integrated Social Work Methods*, George Allen and Unwin, London.

Payne, C J, (1979) United Kingdom: A Children's Centre, in Payne, C J and White K J (eds), *Caring for Deprived Children: International Case Studies of Residential Settings*, RCA, Croom Helm, London.

Payne, C J and White, K J (eds), (1979) *Caring for Deprived Children: International Case Studies of Residential Settings*, RCA, Croom Helm, London.

Perrucci, R, (1974) *Circle of Madness*, Prentice-Hall, Englewood Cliffs NJ.

Petrie, C, (1980) *The Nowhere Boys*, Saxon House, Farnborough.

Pick, P, (1981) *Children at Tree Tops: An Example of Creative Residential Care*, Residential Care Association, London.

Pines, A, Aronson, E and Kafry, D, (1981) *Burnout: From Tedium to Personal Growth*, New York Free Press.

Pines, A and Kafky, D, (1977) Occupational Tedium in the Social Services, *Social Work*, vol 23 No 6, pp 499-507.

Polsky, H W, (1962) *Cottage Six: The Social System of Delinquent Boys in Residential Treatment*, Wiley, London.

Polsky, H W and Claster, D S, (1968) *The Dynamics of Residential Treatment*, University of North Carolina Press, Chapelhill.

Porterfield, J, (1974) Living-In: Help or Hindrance?, *Residential Social Work*, vol 14, No 12, pp 394-395.

Preston-Shoot, M and Braye, S, (1991) Managing the Personal Experience of Work, *Practice*, vol 5, No 1, pp 13-33.

Rasmussen, H C, (1984) New worlds, New challenges, in Philpot, T (ed), *Group Care Practice: The challenge of the next decade*, Community Care, Business Press International, Sutton.

Reed, M, (1977) Stress in Live-In Child Care, *Child Care Quarterly*, vol 6 No 2, pp 114-120.

Robbins, D, (1990) *Child Care Policy-Putting it in Writing: A Review of English Local Authorities' Child Care Policy Statements*, HMSO, London.

RCA, (1980) *A Platform for the 1980's: A New Approach to Training - An Appraisal of Current Training for Residential and Day Care and a Model for the Future*.

Rushforth, M, (1978) *Committal to Residential Care: A Case Study in Juvenile Justice*, HMSO, Edinburgh.

Rowe, J, Hundleby, M and Garnett, L (1989) *Child Care Now: A Survey of Placement Patterns*, British Agencies for Adoption and Fostering, London.

Schaefer, C E and Swanson, A J (eds), (1988) *Children in Residential Care: Critical Issues in Treatment*, Van Nostrand Reinhold, New York.

Seed, P and Thomson, M, (1977) *All Kinds of Care: An Investigation into the Use of Residential and Day Care Facilities for Children in the Highlands and Western Isles of Scotland*, University of Aberdeen.

Seed, P, (forthcoming) *Developing Holistic Education: A Case Study of Raddery School for Emotionally Damaged Children*, Falmer Press.

Staffordshire County Council, (1991) *The Pindown Experience and the Protection of Children*, The Report of the Staffordshire Child Care Enquiry 1990, Staffordshire County Council.

Stainton-Rogers, W, (1988) *Received into Care*, Open University Course D211, Block 3, Open University Press, Milton Keynes.

Stein, M and Carey K, (1986) *Leaving Care*, Basil Blackwell, Oxford.

Stewart, G and Tutt, N, (1987) *Children in Custody*, Avebury, Aldershot.

Stewart, J K, Yee, M D and Brown, R J, (1989) Changing Social Work Roles in Family Centres: A Social Psychological Analysis, *British Journal of Social Work*, vol 20, pp 45-64

Strathclyde Social Work Department, (1984) *Who Are They?*, Strathclyde Regional Council Social Work Department, Glasgow.

Swanson, D, (1987) Stress and Burnout I: The Development of a Taxonomy, *Residential Treatment for Children and Youth*, vol 4 No 3, pp 9-30.

Swanson, M, (1988) Preventing Reception into Care: Monitoring a Short Stay Refuge for Older Children, in Freeman, I and Montgomery, S (eds), *Child Care: Monitoring Practice*, Research Highlights in Social Work 17, Jessica Kingsley Publishers, London.

Thornton, D, Curran, L, Grayson, D and Holloway, V, (1984) *Tougher regimes in Detention Centres: Report of an Evaluation by the Young Offender Psychology Unit*, HMSO, London.

Thorpe, D, Smith, D, Green, D and Paley, J, (1980) *Out of Care: The Community Support of Juvenile Offenders*, George Allen and Unwin, London.

Tizard, J, Sinclair, I and Clarke, R V G, (1975) *Varieties of Residential Experience*, RKP, London.

Triseliotis, J, (1988a) Residential Care from a Historical Perspective, in Wilkinson, J E and O'Hara, G (eds), *Our Children: Residential and Community Care*, National Children's Bureau (Scottish Group), London.

Triseliotis, J, (1988b) An Overview of the Studies, in Freeman, I and Montgomery, S (eds) *Child Care: Monitoring Practice*, Research Highlights in Social Work 17, Jessica Kingsley Publishers, London.

Triseliotis, J and Russell, J, (1984) *Hard to Place: The Outcome of Adoption and Residential Care*, Gower, Aldershot.

Utting, W (1991) *Children in the Public Care: A Review of Residential Child Care*, HMSO, London.

Wagner, G (1988) *Residential Care: A Positive Choice*, Report of the Independent Review of Residential Care, National Institute for Social Work, HMSO, London.

Walter, J A, (1978) *Sent Away: A Study of Young Offenders in Care*, Saxon House, Farnborough.

Walton, R G and Elliot, D (eds), (1980) *Residential Care: A Reader in Current Theory and Practice*, Pergamon Press, Oxford.

Ward, E, (1970) *Follow-up Study of Reading Children from Child Guidance Clinic Treated in Child Guidance Hostels, 1964-69*.

Ward, L (1980) The Social Work Task in Residential Care, in Walton, R G and Elliot, D (eds) *Residential Care: A Reader in Current Theory and Practice*, Pergamon Press, Oxford.

Waterhouse, L, (1989a) In Defence of Residential Care, in Morgan, S and Righton, P (eds), *Child Care: Concerns and Conflicts - A Reader*, Hodder and Stoughton, London.

Waterhouse, L, (1989b) Residential Child Care: Matching Services with Needs, in Morgan, S and Righton, P (eds), *Child Care: Concerns and Conflicts - A Reader*, Hodder and Stoughton, London.

Weber, G H and Haberlein, B J (1972), Problems and Issues in Residential Treatment, in *Residential Treatment of Emotionally Disturbed Children*, Behavioural Publications, New York.

Wiener, (1989), Stress Within the Team, *Social Work Today*, 20(35), pp 20-21.

White, K (1979) United Kingdom: Independent Long Stay Children's Home, in Payne, C J and White, K (eds), *Caring for Deprived Children: International Case Studies of Residential Settings*, RCA, Croom Helm, London.

White, K, (1987), Residential Care of Adolescents: Residents, Carers and Sexual Issues in Horobin, G (ed) *Sex, Gender and Care Work*, Research Highlights in Social Work 15, Jessica Kingsley, London.

White, W L (1978) *Incest in the Organizational Family: The Unspoken Issue in Staff and Program Burnout*, cited in Mattingly (1982), unpublished paper presented at the 1978 National Drug Abuse Conference Seattle, Washington.

Whitebrook, M, Homes, C, Darrah, R and Friedman, J, (1981) Who's Managing the Child Care Worker?: A Look at Staff Burnout, *Children Today*, vol 10 No 1, pp 2-6.

Whittaker, J K, (1981) Major Approaches to Residential Treatment, in Ainsworth, F and Fulcher, L (eds), *Group Care for Children: Concept and Issues*, Tavistock, London.

Whittaker, J K and Trieschman, A E (eds), (1972) *Children Away from Home: A Sourcebook of Residential Treatment*, Aldine, Chicago.

Wilkinson, J E and O'Hara, G (eds), (1988) *Our Children: Residential and Community Care*, National Children's Bureau (Scottish Group), London.

Williams, J (1990) Taking Care of Staff, in Marshall, M, Preston-Shoot, M and Wincott, E, (eds), *Effective Management*, BASW, Birmingham.

Working Party Z, (1969) *Report on Training for Residential Child Care*, Children's Department, Home Office.

Younghusband, E (1978) *Social Work in Britain: 1950-1975 - A Follow-up Study*, vols 1 and 2, George Allen and Unwin, London.

Annex A

Review of Residential Child Care

ORAL EVIDENCE
Mr Ian Baillie - CETSW
Barnardos IT Project, Falkirk parents
Mr R Clough MBE - General Secretary, Social Care Association
Mr Haydn Davies-Jones - Dean of Education
Mr Alan Finlayson OBE- Former Reporter to the Children's Panel, Lothian Region
Mr Peter Hassett - CCETSW
Heads of Inspection Units - Local Authority Social Work Departments
Mrs Barbara Kahan OBE - Chairman, National Children's Bureau
Mr Mike King - Depute Head, Social Work Department, Northern College
Mr Charles Mathers, Children's Rights Officer - Tayside Social Work Department
Mr Tim O'Brien - Workforce Planning and Care Sector Project, COSLA
Mr Peter Ritchie - Consultant
Sister Consolata Smyth RGS - Good Shepherd Centre, Bishopton
Strathclyde Regional Council, Education Department
Training Officers - Local Authority Social Work Departments
Mr Tom White - Chief Executive of National Children's Homes
"Who Cares?" Scotland

WRITTEN SUBMISSIONS
Aberlour Child Care Trust
Associations of Chief Police Officers in Scotland
Association of Directors of Education
Association of Directors of SocialWork
Association of Heads of Scottish Residential Special Schools
Association of Reporters to Children's Panels
Association of Scottish Police Superintendents
Barnardos Scotland
Bridges Project
British Agencies for Adoption and Fostering
British Medical Association
British Paediatric Association
Camphill - Rudolf Steiner Schools
Central Council for Education and Training in Social Work
Childrens Panel Advisory Group
Childrens Panel Advisory Committee - Fife Chairman
Childrens Panel Chairmens Group - Borders Chairman
Childrens Panel Chairmens Group - Grampian Chairman
Childrens Panel Chairmens Group - Lothian Chairman
Convention of Scottish Local Authorities
Director of Public Health - Argyll and Clyde
Director of Public Health - Lothian
Director of Social Work - Fife
Director of Social Work - Grampian
Director of Social Work - Strathclyde
Director of Social Work - Shetland

Edinburgh Council for the Single Homeless
Epoch
Faculty of Public Health Medicine
Glasgow Council for Single Homeless
Health Board General Managers   - Ayrshire & Arran
                                 - Borders
                                 - Dumfries & Galloway
                                 - Fife
                                 - Grampian
                                 - Greater Glasgow
                                 - Highland
                                 - Lanarkshire
                                 - Lothian
                                 - Tayside
                                 - Western Isles
University of Dundee - Professor E Mapstone
University of Edinburgh - Social Work Section
University of Stirling - Miss Helen Kinloch
University of Stirling - Professor C Rowlings & Mr R Fuller
Jordanhill College of Education - Social Work Division
Law Society of Scotland
Moray House College
National Childrens Home
Quarriers Homes
Regional and Islands Reporters Group
Regional Reporters to Childrens Panels - Central
                                        - Fife
                                        - Strathclyde
Rimbleton House - Mr R MacLean - Principal
RSSPCC
Salvation Army
Scottish Association of Citizens Advice Bureaux
Scottish Association of Childrens Panels
Scottish Association of Family Based Respite Care
Scottish Child and Family Alliance
Scottish Child Law Centre
Scottish Council of Independent Schools
Scottish National Commission for Pastoral and Social Care
Scottish Police Federation
Who Cares? Scotland
Woodlands School- Mr P Machell - Principal
Mr F Woods, Principal Psychologist - Child Care Psychology Service

Printed in Scotland for HMSO by (61484)
Dd 287536 C20 11/92.